MW01705012

Thank you Lord for lay leadership! Tom Balderston reminds us that God wants to and can use any of his children to be literary lights in our world. Tom shares intimately the mile-markers of a layman's journey with God—all beautifully woven around the Christmas story. Tom takes us back thousands of years into the history of a Jewish nation, then turns us around and leads us through the life of Christ and on into faith in our often confusing modern-day world. It is here, as Tom shows us, that we all find ourselves at a crossroads as to what we will believe and do with our time on this planet. Read on and enjoy this man's story of how God has touched his heart for all of eternity.

—*Dan Bosko, teaching and connecting pastor, Crossroads Church of Aspen*

WAKE UP! WAKE UP!

The testimony of a Layman

WAKE UP! WAKE UP!

The testimony of a Layman

THOMAS W. BALDERSTON

TATE PUBLISHING & *Enterprises*

Published by Tate Publishing & Enterprises, LLC
127 E. Trade Center Terrace | Mustang, Oklahoma 73064 USA
1.888.361.9473 | www.tatepublishing.com

Tate Publishing is committed to excellence in the publishing industry. The company reflects the philosophy established by the founders, based on Psalm 68:11,
"The Lord gave the word and great was the company of those who published it."

Cover design by Amber Gulilat
Interior design by Joey Garrett

Published in the United States of America

ISBN: 978-1-60799-492-3
Religion / Christian Life / General
09.06.30

Dedicated to You

This book is dedicated to my wife, our children, in-laws, grandchildren, brother, and extended family. May they all find through my faith a renewed or increased conviction in their own Christian belief. To my friends who have walked before me, with me, and past me, thank you, and may you stay on your path and continue to guide and inspire others as well as me. To everyone who reads this book, thank you for considering my work, but more importantly, if not a believer, may you become a fellow believer and find inspiration in the Word. If you do believe, thank you for your indulgence, and bless you; and if you find only a small nugget from this book that can make the truth better understood or provide some clarity, a new idea, or approach, praise God.

Acknowledgments

The process to write, review, and produce this book has been lengthy but informative, constructive, and most enjoyable. But many thanks are needed.

To Sue Brehm, for aiding in the review and copying and binding of multiple drafts for reading by friends and family. In addition, she provided much assistance in the preparation for the editing process.

To my wife, Dee, for being supportive throughout.

To my children, for reading drafts, and the friends who participated in this process also.

To the many authors I have met through the reading of their books, noted in endnotes, and their contributions to the world of understanding and enlightenment for believers and interested parties exploring their faith.

To the many filmmakers who have taken upon themselves the task of presenting stories of the Bible and Bible history, attempting to bring to life the history and capture my mind in a different way and see even more. Each one is an inspiration for the gift of his or her talent and use of such a blessed gift to increase awareness.

To our ministers and pastors, Neely Towe, Steve Woodrow, Dan Bosko, and David Nicholas for their faith, sermons, inspiration, and friendship.

To the men in my Men's Bible Study for sticking with their commitment to weekly meetings and discussions of topics enhancing their faith and their personal relationships with the Lord. This has been and will continue to be a journey, a rewarding journey along a faith-based path.

To those in the summer Bible study I am fortunate to attend, may your continued support and love endure until God calls.

And to our children and grandchildren, who have read or discussed the manuscript, thank you again for your input, and may they discover the depth of the faith of their parents and find a renewal in their own faith. Melisa, Amanda, Kristin, Tommy, Madison, Carter, Mia, William, Owen, Jake, Brooks, and Anne Lane, and not to forget those who may be joining our family in the future, then too children through marriage, Tim, Bryan, and Mike, may you all realize that life is made fuller by your faith in the Lord.

Table of Contents

13 Introduction

25 The Night Before and the Day of Christmas

31 Why Christmas?

39 Love the Gift: a How-To Book

53 The Message

67 What the Old Testament Reveals Historically

85 Along Comes God's Son

93 What Others Believe

103 There Is a God—a Creator

117 Why Easter? The Resurrection

133 Wake Up, Wake Up—Open up to the Cross

141 Many Roads, Same Destination

149 Clarification and Faith

157 Why Is Church Important?

167 Let God Speak to You, and Speak to God through Prayer

181 Now You Know

185 Finding Your Footing

Introduction

It was a December day in Boca Raton, Florida. Holiday decorations were abundant. Like gingerbread house trimmings, lights decorated many of the homes along Eighteenth Street. It was the season. What season? At the mall it appeared the season to shop and remember family and friends, fellow workers, neighbors, the mailman, newspaper delivery man, even the trash collectors. It was the season to not forget to buy. Do not forget to give. Do not forget to decorate. Do not forget the invitations to parties. And for Florida, we needed extra reminders, since the temperature was in the low eighties. Sunny and warm, no snow forecast or ever expected. There were many places other than Florida where snow was being wished for to make the season more joyful. There were cryptic signs displayed of "Joy," "Noel," "50% off," and even, "Too Much Bought for the Christmas Season—Now on Sale!" TV and newspapers were telling stories of vendors dropping the term *Christmas* in favor of *Holiday Season*. Merry holiday! Political correctness had invaded the season to ensure all would be included; no one would be offended. But by what, and why was there a need for such a PC invasion? Almost everywhere you travel at this time of year, there is cause for celebration. This has been the case for well over one thousand years, and for only one reason. I am writing about that reason.

I grew up in a family that had faith as part of daily life. My mother was Lutheran and my father Quaker; however, my mother's faith was the more influential. Although I attended church and participated in church activities, I cannot say I accepted Christ, but then I never rejected Christ either. I have never been so low that I felt a need for earthly salvation, but that does not mean I did not believe in Christ and his dying for man, thus me too. It did not mean that I did not pray for guidance or acceptance or forgiveness. But I did evolve.

St. John's Lutheran Church in Philadelphia, the Mayfair section, is where I got my foundation, was confirmed, and took my first Communion. I can remember many times, seated next to my mother on wooden benches, actually squirming, anxious for the ordeal, the lengthy service, and sermon, to end. We always dressed well, and it seemed every Sunday was a sunny day. While we attended church services, my father prepared Sunday dinner, served by two p.m. every Sunday, and that was something to look forward to. It also gave Mom the day off.

During high school, I associated with others who attended various churches, and with one fellowship group I was actually presented a Bible for reading passages to a congregation of my peers. I still have that Bible from the Mayfair United Presbyterian Church with an inscription and dated May 27, 1956. The Lord was trying to keep me nearby even then. One young lady I dated in college was Catholic. I attended more than a few masses and gained an appreciation for the structure and formality of this religion.

My first marriage was to an Episcopalian, and that was my church and religion, I guess you can say, for all the years of our marriage. Our daughter was an acolyte in St. Paul's Episcopal Church in Riverside, Connecticut. She was confirmed there and took her first Communion at that church. I was introduced, through my first wife, to Neely Towe, an inspirational Congregational Church pastor (Stanwich Congregational Church, Greenwich, Connecticut) and leader who encouraged attendance at *Tres Dias*, a three-day religious retreat. Each of these influences aided in my evolution. Neely also became my spiritual advisor during a vigil at the end days for my first wife. At my home at the time, she conducted small group discussions with close friends and family that helped us deal with a life made too short by cancer. She offered Communion and spoke with and to us all in ways we can never forget and are forever thankful for.

My second marriage, to Dee, only pointed me more in the direction I needed to follow. She too attended *Tres Dias*. Neely Towe presided at our marriage. We moved to Florida and found a church that has been a home for us, Spanish River Church, Boca Raton, and have been guided by the staff there as well as its founder and spiritual leader, the Reverend David Nicholas. We have been fortunate too to be able to enjoy summers in Colorado, in Snowmass Village, which led us to the Crossroads Church in Aspen, led by Pastor Steve Woodrow. Dee, a strong, devoted, and faithful servant of the Lord, keeps me centered and properly focused on developing a personal relationship with God.

My son attended the University of Notre Dame, a Christian on scholarship for golf to a Catholic university. Prior to that, however, he was exposed to significant religious surroundings, attending schools like St. Paul's Lutheran and St. Andrew's Episcopal, as well as the Kanakuk sports camps in Branson, Missouri. He was exposed to the Lord and the Word but was left to his own decisions. Knowing his dad and step mom's feelings and their faith, he gave me two books, texts from the university, that he felt I would find of interest: *The Story of Christianity, Volume 1 and Volume 2*, by Justo L. Gonzalez.[1] He was right. I discovered that the history of the Christian church was most fascinating and eventful. The author was well organized and made a potentially difficult read quite easy; the subject matter was well presented. The referenced texts provided great history and much background on the development of Christianity, both the turmoil and the benefits, the agreements and the disagreements, as well as being most informative on those persons most identified with the growth of Christianity.

The churches we attend today have young congregations and are growing. This certainly seems to buck the trend, with most religions, as reported by the press, losing congregants. The nature of the services presented and the subjects discussed would be contemporary and Bible-based, respectively. Bill Hybel's Willowcreek Church outside Chicago is an example of the typical environment we find most welcoming in which to learn the Word of God and hear the Word of God from the pulpit (but no pulpit, just a stage or lectern). We have found similar churches on travels to areas outside Grand Rapids, Michigan, and even in

Las Vegas. When in New York City, my wife and I try to attend Redeemer Presbyterian, led by Tim Keller, author and gifted teacher/speaker/theologian, held at Hunter College's auditorium. At those churches, presentations combine upbeat praise music with full instrumentation, often with a "rock" tempo, drama, and sermons guided by the Bible and daily life, telling the good news along with the bad. Anyone can attend and not feel limited by not understanding the liturgy or the pattern of worship. Rigid liturgies, visible signs of worship with the use of ornate vestments, and other precious religious elements, are absent. The Catholic or Episcopal Church would be examples of the latter. The Bible is the emphasis of all sermons, and parishioners are encouraged to bring their Bibles and read their Bibles, even take notes. Copies of the sermons are readily available by CD or even iPod downloads.

Spanish River, I must note, with David Nicholas at the helm, has taken upon itself a role as venture capitalist, as it were, to start new churches all over the world. To Reverend Nicholas's credit, more than two hundred facilities have begun, from Haiti and India, to New York City and Seattle, even Puerto Rico and Mexico, and most recently, Croatia and Chad. The theme at all remains similar: the Bible is the foundational text, and from the Word, a relationship with God is established.

As I became more interested in my faith, my wife suggested I read the Bible—not passages, but the Bible—cover to cover. We all seem to read books, but the Bible is not one people generally tend to find engrossing from the perspective of curling up with a good book. However, and fortunately, there are many who view the Bible as the ultimate book for history, guidance, and deliverance. My Bible reading was not a simple task. I was distracted, needed to fill in the tangential elements that arose as I read. I wanted to know more about creation, the locations of events in the Bible, and the *why* of certain happenings. I especially wanted to know more about the seven hundred years before Jesus was born, the frequent battles to conquer all or parts of Israel and Judea, the wars that dispersed the Jews to many parts of the continent and the times the Jews were enabled to return to Jerusalem, the life of Jesus, his crucifixion, resurrection, and the development of the church.

So I read more—books about Herod, the Dead Sea Scrolls, the Assyrians, the Babylonians, Jewish history, the Reformation, and the resurrection; what I would call "feet-on-the-ground" information that made the Bible more real. What I read always seemed to support the dialogue in the Bible and expand upon the history that occurred. Jesus's birth, life, and death were focal subjects in themselves, and so much has been written and discovered archaeologically, geologically, and in historical writings that provides clear evidence that Jesus lived and walked a small area of our earth in a short period of time and yet had a greater influence on mankind—humanity—than any other individual. Not as much has even been written about other fundamental religious leaders, like Muhammad or Buddha. Nor has there been anywhere near the extent of research conducted on another religion with a sizable following.

I read about the life of Paul and the apostles and books just about Jesus also; inspirational books and studies of specific Bible chapters. Then I began reading the controversial books by evolutionists, atheists, and the apologists. I read C.S. Lewis, Lee Strobel, Antony Flew, Sam Harris, Andre Comte-Sponville, N.T. Wright, Beth Moore, Charles Darwin, R.C. Sproul, and Richard Dawkins, among many others; views that were most engaging, at times contentious, even argumentative but also revealing, insightful, inspirational, and objective. My eyes opened wider with each read, and my faith grew, my understanding increased, and I began a much more personal relationship with God. The Bible became more personal. Though God spoke more clearly (metaphorically via the Word), I needed help to see and understand, but then it happened.

I thought the thinking of a layman, an individual, neither philosopher nor scientist (in the PhD or practiced sense), just a believer, one of his sheep, one who took a long time to be 100 percent convinced, might be of interest to someone. In so many respects, I am simply one of the Lord's sheep, but then, too, I am a shepherd. I attended occasional small-group men's Bible studies and then, encouraged by a few, started a Bible study at my home for a group of friends, currently nine brothers in our faith. We have been at it for two years, learning as we go, attempting to answer questions as to our doubts along the way. We started with the Gospel of John then moved to Genesis. This is not a gathering of Bible scholars or a group of devoted Christians, but they have all been willing to study, attend, and grow together. We are progressing. I have been thanked by this group for bringing and keeping them together, but in truth, I may be the greatest beneficiary because the work in preparation takes me to new places of understanding and enlightenment and brings me closer to knowing God.

The research and study I have done, the many books read and discussions held, the many notes taken and thoughts recorded, led me to try my hand at writing, following the evidence and attempting to discuss a variety of issues raised. Every stone or piece of moss uncovered revealed a continued truth that I have tried to explore without too much detail or esoteric commentary. I have tried to remain true to the KISS principle (for those unfamiliar: *Keep It Simple, Stupid*). But to ensure that the reader knows where I am coming from, my personal conclusion remains that God exists and God is, and Jesus is, was, and will be also.

God and Jesus are not humans; no, not at all. They transcend that, but as for God, we may not see him or touch him; but he fills us up with knowledge, the ability to increase our knowledge and understanding, and the understanding of what is right or wrong. And also, we need to make an effort, to take the time to come to gain a fuller appreciation for God's work and the role of God's son, Jesus. But then there is the too-often-misunderstood Spirit, the Holy Spirit. We cannot forget the Spirit, and once my faith in Jesus was known more to me, a realization that I truly believed, then too the Spirit was more apparent. To even consider that the Spirit was in me, inside, an infectious internal mechanism that engendered me to want more, to seek more, and to grow further in my personal relationship and fulfillment of God—God the Father, the Son, and the Holy Spirit, the Triune God—was in itself a revelation.

Now, when it comes to December and the approach of Christmas, I always question the sincerity of those approaching the holiday as a time to celebrate. But celebrate what? It is such a vital time for a Christian. It is such a recognized holiday for the entire world. From China to the United States, Christmas is celebrated and celebrated because it is the time when Christ was born. But many areas where Christmas is celebrated and Christ is known, he is not believed; God is not in first place. The world as it is known is one in which to party, where self is number one, where man places himself above God, and where Christmas is a time to exchange presents. Is it the antichrist at work? Do people even know who the antichrist is? We need to wake up and read the Bible; we need to get together with others and seek knowledge from the Word.

Herein lie my thoughts and personal inspirations, and herein I make a layman's attempt, as a shepherd, or as a shepherd-in-training, to convince others to know more about the reason for Christmas, the person behind Christmas, the gift available to everyone, and the value of the Word of God. Christ is real. God exists. Man was made by God, but God has left man to decide for himself. A man, albeit the son of God, was crucified. Jesus died on the cross as a substitute for the sins of man. The resurrection happened. And if you come to realize that this all happened—it really, really happened—and you then believe, the Spirit will find its way into your heart, and you will find in yourself a rebirth, a renewal of what life is all about, an excitement, and a pleasant association with someone who truly loves you.

A gift was left for all mankind, a guide to life, an irrevocable gift, an indescribable gift—the Word of God, the Bible, a Son, and the hope for an eternal resting place. It is via this gift that a door to understanding and personal salvation is possible. It is the gift that also reminds me of Christmas, but as a believer, Christmas and Christ take on so much more meaning.

But this is not a book about Christmas. It is not a Christmas story, even though I do like the story about the birth of our Savior. It is a testimonial of sorts. I am excited about my faith and my daily thoughts about a life with God. I am encouraged by the spirit within me to continue to learn, but (and this is where the burden also falls on you, the reader) I want you to hear from me—a humble servant, a man of no cloth, but a man of the streets, a businessman, a father, a grandfather, a husband, a friend, an acquaintance, a nobody—my thoughts about what I have discovered and uncovered. I want to share what I have found, do it for you also to share, if indeed you get it. If you get it or already have it, I have succeeded.

Greater minds than mine have addressed this subject, but here a lesser man tries to engage the reader to do what I have done to discover the truth and the lack of deniability of that truth. I am not a reverend, a priest, a pastor, or a Bible scholar. I do not have a PhD in religion. But I have been reading and continue to read; I have done research and continue to do research; I have heard lectures and sermons and continue to do so; I have watched hours of Bible story movies and documentaries, and I believe more today than ever before in the existence of God and the Lord Jesus Christ and his purpose for man and what he has done for man. As I believe, I also believe the Spirit is in me and is encouraging me to do what I can in delivering a message to others.

Take the time—not just the holiday seasons but

any time of the year, for every day is Christmas; every day is Sunday; every day is a day Christ was born. For every day is Easter; every day is a day Christ died for man, suffered more than we will ever suffer and offered an everlasting life that only we can hope to fulfill by believing. Every day is a day Jesus gave himself as a substitute, freeing you and me from our sins and the wrath of God. His resurrection and appearance before throngs provide proof, events that never occurred prior or since. The appearance of Jesus after death in a resurrected state opened the eyes of many, including Paul (the apostle) to his work on earth, his reason for living among us, and actually made it easier to believe and know the truth that has been spoken and written. Do not be afraid to believe. Accept the gift we have all been given (and I mean all, every person on this earth). Immerse yourself in the gift and discover, allow it to open for you, as I have come to realize a wonderful, loving, and caring place does exist. Mankind can be fair, open-minded, objective, and loving. But more people need the gift. More people need to discover the fruits of the Spirit.

Know now that Christmas and Easter speak to us all and remind us all of the life of our Savior. But almost every home has the book somewhere, the Bible on a bookshelf, a countertop, stored as an heirloom from a lost loving relative, has available the written Word; that Word is the living God. Open the gift, assemble it, and put it to the test. You will find you may use it every day. It is the answer to all your questions. It can make the world a better place.

I have found my way and herein share it with you. In my sharing I give you my gift—this book—so you too can see another's view, the view from a free approach to finding God. God is hoping his lost children will return home. I have and have been greeted with open arms.

May this be my present to you! May my random discoveries help you to know also the hope and future that are possible. The gift that keeps giving is the irrevocable gift, the indescribable gift.

The Night Before and the Day of Christmas

> Twas the night before Christmas, when all through the house not a creature was stirring, not even a mouse. The stockings were hung by the chimney with care, in hopes that St. Nicholas soon would be there. [2]

Winter is not the same everywhere, but wherever, it is the season for celebrating Christmas; and there is knowing, an awareness, that this special holiday is upon us all everywhere, in all parts of the world. And as for Christmas Eve, yes, we know that tonight is the evening before a day of much excitement and anticipation, a day for rejoicing and celebration, a day for love and kindness. We prepare for bed and a night of dreams, sugarplums too, with good thoughts only, so it seems, of a day to remember. Then to bed we go, and we sleep; and when tomorrow we wake, the gifts of Christmas appear. There can be so much expectation.

Stockings are named for those to whom they belong; they are filled with small gifts to get the day started and hung in clear view for the early risers to see.

What will it be when morning comes? Who will have been there when daylight shines? Santa Claus is known worldwide, often under various aliases and similar but not exact costuming. His job, however, remains the same. Call him Santa, Kris Kringle (Germany), Pere Noel (France), Papa Noel (Spain), St. Nicholas, Father Christmas, the Jolly Old Elf, Jolly Old Saint Nick, ChristKind (Austria), and more. He delivers the gifts, and stories are told of his exploits, his cadre of elves and other helpers that enable presents to be distributed throughout the world in a most timely fashion, by various means, but primarily sleigh with reindeer. Regardless of the method of delivery or the presents, what we all know is how special a day is Christmas. The world is so different, but the entire world says it remembers the birthday we celebrate that day. It is a birthday party.

The Day

On Christmas Day, we enjoy the decorations and a special breakfast as stockings are taken from the hearth and those little items are opened, and time is occupied while everyone else in the household slowly awakes. We know all the children are ready, so they must be occupied, have something to do, something to unwrap, and something with which to play. There can be heard and seen excitement, squeals of joy, and at times frustration or jealousy over another getting more attention or over whose toy has garnered the attention of another. Sharing is not always as evident as one would like. Squeals of "mine" or expressions of want, even tears and frustration from an over-indulged child, even an adult, may be in evidence. It is all part of the Christmas scene.

A train may pass under the tree, around the gifts, or find a full village scene to travel around. The train setting may have been built with love by a father or grandfather. I'm confident on occasion a mother may have gotten in on the act to ensure a complete experience is realized. There is wonder too in the eyes of many as to the creation of this fun action display and the live railroad passing among the structures or wrapped items. The possible abundance of colorful gift wrappings and moving trains or toy items is viewed positively by young and old alike, and the reactions warm the heart of the wrapper, giver, and creator. There may be small hands trying to divert the path of the locomotive, but only to get closer and be more a part of the action or simply to get at the gifts.

Family

Family is key; it is time for and with family. The best times remembered are when all are together, generations joined, grandparents (in our family it is Mimi and Popsi), parents, children, and grandchildren; uncles and aunts, cousins, and in-laws. The extended family often has a special place at the table. Family members may travel from far and wide to be together all in one place. In the background, as people arrive to the designated home for the family meal, there is a table set with all the elements for a fine meal, and noticeable is the number of seats telling how many will be reaching for the turkey or ham or main dish on that festive occasion.

Food

Meals, meals, meals, indeed a day for meals—a day to consume and enjoy all the good food offerings of the day. A breakfast casserole—my favorite—eggs with sausage and many secret ingredients, along with a Kringle[3] from Wisconsin, heated and indulged along with a fine cup of coffee or tea. Then there is the smell of tea—that special recipe or blend—her favorite, loose Earl Grey Blue tip and just the right blend of mulling spices to make that perfect cup or pot.

Lunch too, after the gifts are unwrapped and torn or ripped wrapping paper is piled about and the debris is discarded and the living or family room is made somewhat presentable. Lunch is generally catch-as-catch-can, make your own, for those who somehow did not get enough during the seemingly all-morning breakfast buffet. Then there is dinner.

Dinner may and can certainly be special in itself. Those who enjoyed Christmas Day at home with their children may now travel to grandparents' or parents' or in-laws' or friends' houses for the big meal of this glorious day. Families travel to or visit from, and a larger gathering builds for a table of ham, turkey, king crab, stone crab, a feast of favorites, cultural specialties, candied yams and mashed potatoes, special sauces, and great desserts, too many, too sweet, and with ice cream.

Oh and about desserts. This is a specialty of my wife: dessert pies. She makes many for this holiday (and just about all holidays) for family and friends. There were at least thirteen or fourteen pie shells made from scratch in our kitchen this year, with subsequent fillings for apple pie, pumpkin pie, lemon cream pie, banana cream pie, and her specialty, pecan pie. Neighbors accustomed to receiving her pies in the past would anxiously await a call to pick up or expect delivery of a freshly baked pie just for them.

The assembled mass for dinner, while waiting, might be observing the beautifully set table, observing the perfect decorations. A festive look in red and green, often with sparkling lights of white, garland of green, needles of pine, pinecones, and the room filled with the wonderful aromas of the day. The gifts, received or exchanged, are available and shared for inspection purposes only. Some may be watching sports or outside playing with a new sled, skis, snowboards, or golf club (area of the country depending), or flying a kite or launching a rocket. I've seen all that and so much more.

The Gathering

So on Christmas Day, children may have brought their favorite toy of the day with them and might be playing indoors with cars, trucks, and dolls, or outdoors. And for the technologically inclined, iPods or iPhones or computer-animated games or game consoles with two or more facing off in battle, controllers in hand. But all fun, and generally, all children make the day meaningful and memorable.

Dinner finds everyone around the table, eating and drinking and laughing and smiling and loving. Champagne and white and red wine flow. Everyone eats too much. The dessert display irresistible and waded into by all. It is a special day. Always a special day.

More time needs to be spent by families gathered around a dinner table, and not just on a special day, but every day possible.

And why do we remember or celebrate? Why is this day, Christmas Day, so special? Christmas was the catalyst to finally taking my gained knowledge and the impact my exploration into the Word of God has had on me and making this attempt to have others make the effort, take a similar approach to knowing the God of the Old and the New, especially the New Testament. And gifts, they are so much a part of that time of year, and my story is about gifts; and herein we continue to discuss the gifts I have opened. I pray many more will be offered to open and continue to fill me with a greater understanding and relationship with the triune God.

Why Christmas?

And there were shepherds living out in the fields nearby, keeping watch over their flocks at night. An angel of the Lord appeared to them, and the glory of the Lord shone around them, and they were terrified. But the angel said to them, "Do not be afraid. I bring you good news of great joy that will be for all the people. Today in the town of David a Savior has been born to you; he is Christ the Lord. This will be a sign to you: You will find a baby wrapped in cloths and lying in a manger."

Luke 2:8-12

An E-mail Received

One year, not long ago, just prior to Christmas, I received an e-mail. This e-mail was sent to several friends, and it appeared the recipients were men. But it had an impact on me. The e-mail follows:

Gentlemen and your Families:
Merry Christmas. Thanks be to God for his

indescribable gift. Do you remember the gift you received last year? I know I can't, but I'm still trying. But then the Christmas story is about salvation. Are we each right with the Lord? We are all justified by his grace. Let us remember this day, Christmas Day, and all days where our heart should be. Let him be the center of your life, and his gift to you will never be forgotten. A good read: Titus 3:4-8.

Make it a most memorable Christmas. Happy New Year too.

Your friend in Christ

The language that struck me was, "Do you remember the gift you received last year?" I thought about neckties, handkerchiefs, a golf shirt, golf balls, and there were family photos, albums of the grandchildren, and many other useful and pleasing items for which I was thankful. But was that really the question? But then it continued: "I know I can't, but I'm still trying." That was insightful, for what was I forgetting? I must be forgetting something. But then it hit me. The electronic transmission reminded me—why Christmas? And the why starts the day, *Christ*mas. Not hidden, obvious, but then again, not so obvious. How often we forget the true gift of Christmas.

A Special Someone

Whatever our religion, whatever we believe, whatever our faith, everyone knows that someone named Jesus is revered this day called Christmas (by many). It was around the time of his birth. *Happy Birthday, Jesus*! Jesus makes the gifts possible. Some know his gift. Some do not. Some don't care. But all are aware. Fewer than two hundred miles from birth 'til death (thirty to thirty-one years) were traveled by Jesus, and look at his reach: the entire world. He touched us all, some more directly and others made aware, some in awe, others despair, some in love, others in hate; but whatever his fate, he made his mark, and the whole world remembers in its own way. Who else, may I ask, is so remembered? There just must be a reason for all of this. For "the earth will be full of the knowledge of the Lord as the water covers the sea" (Isaiah 11:9b).

On Christmas morning, wives get special gifts from husbands, husbands from wives, girlfriends from boyfriends, boyfriends from girlfriends, children, good and bad, are given toys and gadgets and clothes and games and, and, and. Relatives exchange gifts. Friends exchange gifts. And so on. Everyone is so giving, giving to others and with heartfelt kindness and joy. Gifts are given out of love. Yes, out of love. For he so loved the world. Wow, good stuff. It is a remembrance of the gift we have all been offered, all been given.

The Music

Think about the music of the season, for what day of the year are there as many songs written? Is it Hanukkah, Kwanzaa, or Christmas? The winner is . . . Christmas! "I'm Dreaming of a White Christmas," "Frosty the Snowman," "Rudolph the Red-Nosed Reindeer," "The

First Noel," and "Silent Night." There are hundreds of songs, and various musicians and vocalists record many of the same songs.

Is this a day to rejoice, or what? For some it is a day, in fact a season leading to the day, to profit. Yes, and the greater the profit, the greater the rejoicing. Even nonbelievers may rejoice if they make goods and provide services others purchase for this day. For some businesses, retail especially, it is this time of year that they make whatever money and profits that they plan, expect, or hope for the entire year.

Memories

But it is the special times, the memories, that all will remember. A holiday enjoyed, a dinner with family, direct and/or extended, a church service, and a delighted face of one receiving an unexpected gift or sentiment, a failed or troubled trip to visit family, friends, or loved ones celebrating together; these all provide memories. Yes, we all prefer to share this day in some way with someone. Even if it is the person with whom we may share the profits. Getting together and rejoicing is a byword of the day that is Christmas.

Service to Others

I remember a wonderful family. They did not believe in Jesus, and they claimed they did not believe in Christmas; and they did not celebrate. In fact, they worked on

Christmas—the entire family, including the children from the time they were old enough—in service to others as preparers and/or servers at a family dinner. Even though they did not celebrate and claimed they did not believe, they knew the reason for Christmas. They understood that this day meant so much to so many. Was their service a service to the Lord? We will never know, but they served willingly and enthusiastically.

There are those who celebrate Christmas even though they do not believe. Many may claim they do it for the children. It is a holiday, a nation's holiday, many a nation's holiday, a world holiday, a work holiday; why not celebrate? But the focus of this day is seldom forgotten, and even for those who may not believe, at some point they may ask or question the day. Is Jesus at work every Christmas reminding the world? I say *yes*.

The Worst of Times

Christmas may not always be the best of times for some. My first wife died just after Christmas 1989. All through the holidays she was dying, and a vigil was held at our home for those to visit, meet, pay their respects, and see her or speak with her for the last time. She was unable to speak, but there was communication. It was possible to elicit a smile or a nod. She was loved, and her health issue was tragic; but it was her time.

Life is not all good news; there is bad news too. I may have provided a joyous picture of Christmas (and that is the image I prefer), but depression and remorse can befall many. It is dealing with the trauma, life's dilemmas and frustrations, but remembering the reason for the season and what it can provide for all through reflection. I am not saying it is easy or suggesting that when down or suddenly alone or when you question God, an unhappy outcome, you simply splash cold water on your face, have a stiff upper lip, or get over it because life goes on, for there is a time for suffering, for remorse. It took me time, I know, and there are still moments, especially at holiday time, when I feel some sadness, especially for the short life of a vital, beautiful, talented, forty-four-year-old woman and mother of my children. I will admit too that at the time I was not as strong in my faith as I am today, but you should know my faith was strengthened.

There were so many caring people who came into my life, caring people I hardly knew. A prayer group met twice a week at our home to accommodate my wife, but helpful to so many, with Communion celebrated each week. All were welcome. The Communion was simple: a loaf of bread, a bottle of wine, and each person faced his neighbor as the elements were passed and said, "Take, eat…" and then, "Take, drink…" repeating the words of a local minister who graced us each week to conduct each prayer session. Tears were shed, embraces were made, love was felt, a presence in the room. Men and woman had lunch with me and shared their feelings, providing comfort and solace. Meals were provided, a list prepared and organized with assignments made to deliver on each night. This continued months after her death.

All I can say and have often reflected on is that without our community and God, it would have been so much more difficult. In time I overcame the grief and did move forward, but my life was different; my goals were different, and my faith was different. I was more thankful and certainly more appreciative of what people can and are willing to do. I wanted to change and understand what it is that causes people to act on what they feel. It may have been my epiphany, but I will tell you this: the next day I did not go and profess my faith; that took more time.

Decorate Your Heart

But no matter how bad it may be, remembering a father sacrificing his only son for us all should provide some insight, some comfort, knowing that we are not alone in our trials or our pain. The man we celebrate at Christmas suffered also and suffers with us, but he also celebrates with us as well. Still, I find difficulty with the season, but more from the excesses and the burdens placed upon many to make something of this time of year than from the true cause of this time, this memory.

Buy a tree, decorate a tree, put up lights, take from storage past years' decorations, and begin anew to make your place a showcase for Christmas, and know too that when it is over, the reverse must happen. The tree comes down, along with the lights, the decorations are packed and stored for next year, and the piles of trash that are generated need to be removed. There is a lot of work involved. But with or without the work, it is not the appearance of Christmas, the media reminders, keeping up with the neighbors or friends—it is your heart, how you decorate your heart.

Decorate your heart with love. Be kind, gentle, caring, giving (not monetarily necessarily), and temperate. Be a beacon for those who remember the birth that is celebrated. Let the Holy Spirit within you shine. Then the effort will be worthwhile, and whatever is done to decorate or prepare will be sufficient. Back to the e-mail: "The Christmas story is about salvation."

To Know More

Did Jesus do all of this? Yes! Is this his way of introducing his message? Yes! The greatest gift of all—a kingdom on earth, good versus evil, light versus darkness. Everyone has a choice to do the right thing. You too have the gift.

Let us all, for a moment anyway, enjoy. Give God and Jesus a moment of your time to consider what took place to create this day called Christmas—a day special to so many.

There is much we all need to know and understand. There is the who, what, and why of Christmas. For those who believe and have such faith, why has this day become such a worldwide tradition, and how do we ensure the true message of the day is heard? The message of Christmas, what is it? It is Jesus's message! Why should we not know more about it?

And the e-mail ended, "Let us remember this day, Christmas Day, and all days where our heart should be. Let him be the center of your life, and his gift to you will never be forgotten. And so I was inspired and reminded. And I am writing to you now to remind you too, to inspire you. Get to know and love the Lord."

Love the Gift: A How-To Book

My child, hear my Words, Words of the greatest sweetness, surpassing all the learning of the philosophers and the wise of the world.[4]

The previous chapter closed by suggesting we get to know God better. The process for me involved reading, and the big step was reading the Bible. And to get to know God, that really is the way to start. What could be better? Begin by reading what was written by messengers, witnesses, and apostles of the Lord. You will get to experience history, places, and developments and be enlightened and delighted by what you learn.

What a challenge. Read the Bible from cover to cover. It was quite an experience for me. Or I should say, it *is* quite an experience, since it continues to this day. Just about every day I read a portion of the Bible; it may be just a few lines or most of a chapter. Something strikes a chord, makes me think about a passage, or a situation occurs that causes me to find an answer or the right thing to say in the Word. I have not been disappointed yet. It is like Ask.com: you go to the reference, and you find an answer to your question.

My initial attempt took over a year. I was often confused or had questions and began to search elsewhere for added clarity, historical evidence, confirmation from another source, or just to learn more about the topic that was presented that for me just needed more detail. I was successful each time. My interest and enjoyment grew. The Old Testament is a difficult read, and remembering all the kings and the tribes of Israel, where and when they came and went, was quite a task. Also, how God was presented took a bit of work to fully comprehend and appreciate. Creation: okay, I got it, but was it successful? Did God achieve his end, especially with Adam's error? Why the Jews, the chosen people, and all their trials and tribulations and their errors too?

The Old Testament and the New Testament are quite different. The God in the New seems different in some ways from the God of the Old. I know they are both God, but with the New, we now have Jesus and the Holy Spirit. Most of what occurs in the New is forecast in the Old and often in ways that tell the Jews that there will be consequences for their actions. There is a lot crammed into sixty-six books and one thousand or so pages (depending on the font and the footnotes). The Old and the New, however, go together, and in the New there are changes, a means for the mistakes of the Old to be corrected in the form of a new covenant or a new creation. God, his Son, and the Spirit work as a team to transform man, everyone, into being part of that team to make the world the heaven on earth God planned.

The Gift of Love

The gift of Jesus, of God, is love. And the answers to all questions can be found in one place, one source—the Bible. How simple is that, a how-to source? The Bible is the Word of God, God-breathed[5], for all to read and understand. Admittedly, it is not an easy read. But it is worth the effort, the time, and the dedication because it will open the reader's eyes to a life that is good. There are many metaphors, some conflicting elements, but taken as a whole, it shows why all people are today, and have been since the birth of Christ Jesus, God's children. If asked whether some passages as written actually happened, is that the way it all took place (literally), I must admit I cannot answer, but what I can say is that they are true, helpful, and powerful messages.

Seeing God

The Bible is a way of seeing God. It is the means by which God speaks to us every day. God comes to us via the Bible. Conditions of our lives, situations that occur, are addressed by the Bible and by God speaking to us through the Word. Scripture is all encompassing. The Bible is not an exclusive document; it was written for everyone.

Most people read books, some more often than others. My wife reads more than a book a week. But how many of you have read the Bible? It is the biggest seller of all time, written in just about every language and with various translations. The different translations and writings attempt to make the Bible more readable, more understandable, and more widely available to greater numbers of people. It is a resource that has found a way to be there for everyone. Have you read it? If you have time to read a daily newspaper or a book, set aside just fifteen minutes each day to read the Bible. Read the Bible, and the gift becomes more apparent and more readily available.

There are so many stories, so much advice, poetry, odes, songs, and guiding principles. It is a joy to read, and the impact it will have on you as reader cannot be fully appreciated until you yourself get involved with and captured by the Word of God. A few examples follow.

Stories

There are many stories such as Adam and Eve, Noah and the Ark, Joseph and the Coat of Many Colors, Daniel in the Lion's Den, The Tower of Babel, Jonah and the Whale, The Exodus, The Handwriting on the Wall, The Good Samaritan, The Golden Rule, The Wedding at Cana (Water into Wine), A King is Born (the birth of Jesus), The Three Wise Men, Five Loaves and Two Fish, the Crucifixion, and more and more. The stories of the Bible provide knowledge and understanding and serve to guide readers toward knowing God and his purpose.

Many movies that have been produced, and books written also, have as plots stories from the Bible, from adulterous affairs to battles to father-son relationships, to hardship and suffering, and many love stories, all modified and told in today's environment or reflect on situations that actually happened, having a biblical connection. Stories of love, hope, faith, success, failure, perseverance, and so on, have biblical connections—maybe not directly, but the ideas can usually be traced in many ways back to Bible verses.

Advice

The Bible offers proverbs filled with words of wisdom and advice.

> Let love and faithfulness never leave you; bind them around your neck, write them on the tablet of your heart. Then you will win favor and a good name in the sight of God and man. Trust in the Lord with all your heart and lean not on your own understanding; in all your ways acknowledge him, and he will make your paths straight. Proverbs 3:3-6

Poetry

Poetry can be found throughout the Bible. The Psalms provide a multitude of examples. One that most readers will know or have heard of is Psalm 23.

> The Lord is my shepherd, I shall not be in want. He makes me lie down in green pastures, he leads me beside quiet waters, he restores my soul. He guides me in paths of righteousness for his name-

> sake. Even though I walk through the valley of the shadow of death, I will fear no evil, for you are with me; your rod and your staff, they comfort me. You prepare a table before me in the presence of my enemies. You anoint my head with oil; my cup overflows. Surely goodness and mercy will follow me all the days of my life, and I will dwell in the house of the Lord forever. Psalm 23

Odes

An example of an ode from the Bible can be found in 1 Corinthians.

> Love is patient, love is kind. It does not envy, it does not boast, it is not proud. It is not rude, it is not self-seeking, it is not easily angered, it keeps no record of wrongs. Love does not delight in evil but rejoices with the truth. It always protects, always trusts, always hopes, always perseveres. 1 Corinthians 13:4-7

A Toast

To celebrate a friendship, a toast, from Song of Songs 5:

"Eat, O friends, and drink; drink your fill, O lovers."

Songs

Many songs have been inspired by the Bible and its many meanings. But the greatest songs are about love. There is a book of the Bible, Song of Songs, that provides many words of love. Interpretations made compare the love of wisdom to that of the love of a woman and a man and a woman. Well worth a read.

Guiding Principle

And as for guiding principles, they too are throughout the Bible. Again, we turn to Proverbs:

> A man who lacks judgment derides his neighbor; a man of understanding holds his tongue. A gossip betrays a confidence, but a trustworthy man keeps a secret. For lack of guidance a nation falls, but many advisers make victory sure. Proverbs 11:12-14
>
> If you falter in times of trouble, how small is your strength. Proverbs 24:10

Familiar Phrases or Idioms

- Stairway to heaven (Genesis 28:12)
- For the wages of sin is death (Romans 6:23)
- Make swords into plowshares (Isaiah 2:4)
- Man does not live on bread alone (Deuteronomy 8:3)

- Be fruitful and multiply (Genesis 1:28)
- East of Eden (Genesis 3:21)
- Adam's rib (Genesis 2:21)
- Blessed are the peacemakers (Matthew 5:9)
- As old as Methuselah (Genesis 5:25)
- Jacob's ladder (Genesis 28:12)
- Land of milk and honey (Exodus 3:8)
- The meek will inherit the earth (Psalms 37:11)
- Strangers in a strange land (1 Peter 2:11)
- Let my people go (Exodus 5:1)
- Eye for an eye and a tooth for a tooth (Matthew 5:38)
- Jezebel (Esther 4:14)
- Queen of Sheba (1 Kings 10:1)
- Wisdom of Solomon (1 Kings 4:29)
- The patience of Job (from the Book of Job)
- Leviathan (Isaiah 27:1)
- Spare the rod and spoil the child (Proverbs 13:24)
- The skin of my teeth (Job 19:20)
- Welcome the little children (Mark 9:37)
- Forty days and forty nights (Genesis 7:12)
- The floodgates of heaven (Genesis 7:11)
- The Golden Rule (Luke 6:31)
- Much will be demanded from those who have been given much (Luke 12:48)

- A voice calling in the desert (Luke 3:4
- Wolf in sheep's clothing (Matthew 7:15)
- Salt of the earth (Matthew 5:13)
- Go the extra mile (Matthew 5:41)
- Daniel in the lion's den (Daniel 6:7)
- The poison of vipers is on their lips (Romans 3:13)
- A time for war and a time for peace (Ecclesiastes 3:8)
- On earth peace to men (Luke 2:14)
- Turn the other cheek (Matthew 5:38)
- Sodom and Gomorrah (Genesis 19:24)
- Weeping and gnashing of teeth (Matthew 8:12)
- Den of thieves (Mark 11:17)
- Good and faithful servant (Matthew 25:21)
- Physician, heal thyself (Luke 4:23)
- Cast the first stone (John 8:7)
- Stand your ground... stand firm (Ephesians 6:14)
- Written on their hearts (Romans 2:15)
- The handwriting on the wall (Daniel 5:5)
- The kiss of Judas (Mark 14:45)
- Walk on water (Matthew 14:29)
- Greater love hath no man than this (John 15:13)

- Death, where is thy sting (1 Corinthians 15:55)
- The root of all evil (1 Titus 6:10)
- Light of the world (Matthew 5:14)
- The light of life (Psalm 56:13)
- The seventh seal (Revelation 8:1)
- In the twinkling of an eye (1 Corinthians 15:51-52)
- I am the Alpha and Omega (Revelation 1:8)
- Fight the good fight (1 Titus 1:18)
- Armageddon (Revelation 16:16)
- Holier than thou (Isaiah 65:5)
- Sheep, gone astray (Isaiah 53:6)
- As a hen gathers her chicks under her wings (Luke 13:34)
- Wipe away every tear (Revelation 7:17)
- Woe is me! (Isaiah 6:5)
- Can a leopard change his spots? (Jeremiah 13:23)
- A drop in the bucket (Isaiah 40:15)
- Eat, drink, and be merry (Ecclesiastes 8:15)
- Give up the ghost (Job 14:10)
- Am I my brother's keeper? (Genesis 4:9)
- Fat of the land (Genesis 45:18)
- A lamb for the slaughter (Isaiah 53:7)
- The blind leading the blind (Matthew 15:14)

- Old wives' tales (1 Timothy 4:7)
- Soar on wings like eagles (Isaiah 40:31)
- From the lips of children (Matthew 21:16)
- Written in the Book of Life (Revelation 20:15)
- Four corners of the earth (Revelation 20:8)
- Brotherly love (Romans 12:10)
- The Spirit is willing, but the body is weak (Matthew 26:41)
- Busybodies (2 Thessalonians 3:1;Titus 5:13)
- Jars of clay (2 Corinthians 4:7)
- Potter's field (Matthew27:7)
- A household divided against itself will not stand (Matthew 12:25)

So much of our language today contains words, idioms, and phrases from the Bible, and most do not realize the source. "Surely ignorance of the Bible is bound to impoverish one's appreciation of English literature?"[6] And the writer of the prior quote is an atheist.

Gift of Love

To repeat, the greatest gift we all receive, with Christmas and Easter as the reminder—Christians, Muslims, Jews, Buddhists, Hindus, men and woman of all religions, even those without a religion—is the gift of love, the word of God, the pathway and trail map to the kingdom of God. And that kingdom is here on earth. If God were king, then life on earth would be his kingdom. Justice would be his justice. The world would be a better place. The Bible contains all the stories we need to know and understand to discover and develop a relationship with the Lord.

The gift of love is inherent in being a Christian, having faith, having a communion and relationship with the *one*, the God, who created us. With the gift once received or accepted, the Spirit of the Lord takes over, takes up residence within the believer, and allows and enables growth in a loving, peaceful, objective, and open religion. You can even leave the faithful, yet be embraced when you return and loved when you are away.

"The Word was intended by God to be intelligible, and only as we understand does it get into our bloodstreams and into our hearts and show up in changed lives."[7]

"The Bible contains the most profound philosophy, the most perfect morality, and the most refined policy, that was ever conceived on earth."[8]

To close this chapter I reference a question raised by N.T. Wright: "What happens when the gospel takes root?" His answer:

> It happens again and again, thank God: people discover, firing up within themselves, the sense that it does make sense, that they really believe it, that they find it transforming the way they are thinking and feeling about all sorts of other things, that the presence of Jesus is suddenly a reality for them, that reading the Bible becomes

> exciting, that they can't get enough of Christian worship and fellowship.[9]

Part of my testimony is that for me, the conversion was slow, belabored in fact; but it did occur, and what Bishop Wright has said in the afore-noted quote is true. Once you begin to explore and discover and understand, you become an inspired reader, a seeking believer wanting to know more about God, the triune God, and the role you can play, how you can use your talents, and how you can help transform the world while one awaits his future. Interestingly enough, Bishop Wright concludes, and I concur, "those who believe the gospel have no choice but to follow." [10]

The Message

Faith comes from hearing the message, and the message is heard through the word of Christ. Romans 10:17

> All these toys were never intended to possess my heart, that my true good is in another world and my only real treasure is Christ.[11]

There are many messages provided for a reader of the Word. They can be confusing at times; there are possible mixed messages and certainly straightforward messages. When mixed, I explored other writers' thoughts or interpretations to obtain a better understanding. When straightforward, I just went with the flow; there are many that suggest a literal interpretation is the way and others, metaphorical. Well, the former, the literal interpretation, may be straightforward and the latter, the metaphorical, mixed. For some, the messages could be either or both. I may have you totally confused, but bear with me.

Take the seven days of creation. Was it seven days as we know it? I say probably not; it was seven days as God knows it. That leads to a metaphor; the seven days could have been seven million years, a time span that had a different clock from that of today. After all, Adam, had he stuck with eating of the fruit of the tree of life, was to live forever. It seems there were many trees safe from which to eat. But there was one, the tree of good and evil, or the tree of the knowledge of good and evil, that to consume the fruit would really mess things up. It might make you smarter, but no longer would you live forever. Was life to be physical and spiritual and once the wrong fruit was eaten, physical life and the spiritual were made separate? Genesis, the first book, alone contains so much more than I ever imagined, and Christ's presence can be found throughout. The reader doesn't have to wait for the New Testament. But interestingly enough, the clarity of the Bible is not always evident on a first reading. For me it took much more than the first reading. Bible studies have been invaluable.

My first men's Bible study was in Connecticut, after my wife died. About twelve of us gathered in a small room at a nearby club, of which most were members. To begin, our first choice was not the Bible, but the book *Mere Christianity*, by C.S. Lewis. It was as a book club, but with a prayer before and after. God must have had a hand in the selection, for it turned our hearts and minds toward believing. Occasionally, a minister would be asked to give us some guidance. We did not want one as our leader, feeling he or she would dominate. I now know they would have also been helpful, instructive, and possibly made us more efficient in our quest.

One question had to do with *faith*. Boy, we had questions, and most questions or suggestions made just having faith a question in its own right. Our visiting minister was someone we all trusted. We knew the person was a scholar of the Bible and capable of providing unique insight with compassion, love, and an acceptable perspective. After hearing our statements surrounding the question, the answer was simply, "You must just have faith!" In retrospect, that was a fine answer, not the one wanted at the time, but looking back, having faith made understanding the Word easier and clearer. It enabled the Word to speak to us all.

C.S. Lewis made a transition from a lawyer, possibly an atheist, to a strong Christian who devoted much of his life and skillful writing and brilliance to enhancing the reason for and the value of faith, being a faithful servant of the Lord. For all of the men, having faith, just a hint of faith, avoiding denial, accepting what we did not understand, enabled us to move forward, and as we all did so, understanding came. It was like an old masterpiece, an oil painting that had been kept in a basement and over time, with dust and neglect, lost its brilliance and definition. On first glace, it was worthy of only being discarded as a worthless piece of art. But taking the time to clean, refurbish, and make clear different areas, its value, the treasure of the work itself, became more apparent. So too the Bible can do that and reveal the message God wants us all to hear and understand.

A Clear Message

The message of Jesus is clear and made clearer when time is spent with God, his Word, and your heart. To know God and his Son is to know yourself and know too and try hard to do the good, the expected, and the right thing so our kingdom on earth is a secure and comfortable place for everyone. Neither power nor wealth nor poverty nor gifts nor charity nor knowledge ensure God's acceptance. Only an open and willing heart and mind, to let him in, to be your guide, to provide you answers, and to be applied in your life, will find the assurance we all want. To paraphrase Jesus's statement in the New Testament book of John, 21:15, "If you love me, feed my sheep." God wants man to serve others, to be a leader, and bring people, his "sheep," to the Word so they may also drink, eat, and enjoy what God has provided. And so they may also live in his "light."

"If we walk in the light, as he is in the light, we have fellowship with one another" (1 John 1:7).

Jesus's Message

The more you learn about Jesus—his life and his relationships—the more you will learn that his message is about humility and love. Jesus had more power than anyone yet did not use it to make himself appear great. We see today authority as power and power over others as providing authority. We can all learn from Jesus. In our own lives, we may find elements of control that are deemed important to our stature, our success, even as evidence of our accomplishments. But what happens when the power disappears?

Jesus was the Son of God; he came to be with man as man and lived among us. Knowing we are all sinners (and I still fight the battle of my sinful nature daily), Jesus led a perfect life and showed us how. He then died on the cross, sacrificed himself so we have a chance. It is impossible not to err. When those errors are against God, they may be classified as crimes. We are criminals in God's eyes, but God's love shining through his Son gave us freedom and forgiveness. God gave his Son; his Son made the sacrifice. He was punished for our crimes—the crimes of man committed yesterday, today, and tomorrow—and saved us from God's punishment. This is the good news. The bad news is that we all commit heinous acts against God; we steal from him, we disobey him, we push him aside, we do not honor him or worship him, and so much more, and yet he allowed his Son to take the punishment we deserve. For our crime, Jesus did the time.

A retired CEO may find life as a retiree most difficult, not having his minions underfoot. Coping becomes an issue. A Florida country club that catered to successful businessmen found on many an occasion their board of directors was comprised of retired executives from many different industries—finance, food service, retail, advertising, and others—self-made men. It always appears a proper fit with knowledgeable representatives capable of guiding the club's staff and formulating policies beneficial to all, with all that industry experience to bring to the table. They enjoyed the golf, the amenities, and the social life, but on more than one occasion, they discovered in the board room a chance to reign anew over a staff and a business. Micromanagement, changing a governing body into a managing body, and failing to instill in the club's management a sense of ownership in its own decisions, led to problems. Over fifteen years, the club had more than six managers. The board found fault with them all. Yet never was blame cast upon the governing body, but it was the want for power and the lack of humility that caused the problem. It was the board itself that took away the esteem of the managers and ended up with people who had no incentive, no desire to continue under a regime of absolute control. That was not Jesus's style.

Think about your power, small or large. How do you deal with it, even if it is just power over your children? We learn the message from the Bible and from the Lord. What would you do, or how would you react if your power was threatened, if someone came along and directly or indirectly caused some or all to question your power or authority? Do you acquiesce? Do you resist? Do you take action to prevent or stop the threat? What if the threat is perceived, not real, or represents an opportunity in itself? There are so many questions; there is so much to consider or dream about. If you could, would you use any means possible to keep your power? Would you solicit support for your position? Would you incite a riot? Would you use force? Take out the resistance leader? Remove the heart of the threat? The abusive use of power is an act of aggression against God.

Jesus could have controlled the situation he was in but chose a more humble outcome. He did not exercise his power to put down the aggression that was against only him. He had a higher calling. With love and a humble spirit, we too can overcome many challenges and provide more leadership than thought. It is by the example given us by Jesus that we can learn and grow and act and do so for the glory of the Lord, not for ourselves.

> Let us not become weary of doing good, for at the proper time we will reap a harvest if we do not give up. Therefore, as we have opportunity, let us do good to all people, especially to those belonging to the family of believers. Galatians 6:9-10

Wealth

Is his message about wealth? It's not a bad thing. It is what you do with it that matters. Does it make you happy? Are you in it for the money? Are you thankful for your success? The gifts you have, do you use them also for the Lord in some way? Does money make you a better person, better than those without money? Do you want or need more? Can you live with less? Do you worship money? That is not a good thing. How do you share your wealth, your success? Has a quest for money, more of it, as much as can be accumulated, interfered with honoring God?

"You cannot serve both God and Money" (Matthew 6:24b).

The Underprivileged

Is his message about the underprivileged? Are we doing enough to help others? Do we need help ourselves? Does the system meet our needs or the needs of others? Is there fairness in the world? Equality? Are we personally focused on the right things? Are we charitable? Do we do enough for others? Are we compassionate?

Is our self-absorbed nature a wrongful way of dealing with others? Are we disobeying our Lord?

His Influence

Jesus, in his limited travels, had a considerable influence on people; powerful people, wealthy people, but others too, those without means, the infirmed, the poor, the downtrodden. He served the people and always did good. Always doing good, that alone would be a threat to some. Word traveled of miracles he performed as a healer or provider. He gave people a choice, to believe in him or not. Simply believing and acting as he did, the world would be a better place. He was not seeking power, just being an example of how to live, to care, and to give. He was not forcing people to believe in him or follow him. He was not in it for the money; he was poor. He relied on others for housing and food. The only requirement of others was to be an example, as he was an example, and be guided by what is right. Lead by example, not by power or by taking advantage of one's position or by bribery or by absolute control, but by being and doing what is right, helpful, healing, and forgiving and doing so in a loving way.

Jesus's Time on Earth—4 B.C. to 33 C.E.

In Jesus's time, Judah and Israel were under the control of the Romans. For hundreds of years, Jews had been overridden and forced to leave the area they claimed as their birthright. Some returned when the opportunity arose, having been exiled in Assyria, Persia, Babylon, and many areas around, mostly the eastern Mediterranean. Ever since Israel and Jerusalem were invaded and besieged by the Assyrians, in the years 743-701 B.C., the Jews found their home base destroyed or overridden repeatedly.

Why were the Jews displaced so? Why were the key people, the leaders at various times, removed from their country, replaced by the conquerors' select, only remnants to remain? Persons and leaders such as Daniel, Ezra, and Nehemiah were taken to other lands. If not taken, they or their heirs were murdered, or in the case of Zedekiah, blinded (by Nebuchadnezzar). The remnants, those remaining, were then to be controlled by the invaders, the people they brought in as replacements. What did the Jews do to cause all this?

Simply, they did not obey God. They were not faithful to God. God was continually frustrated by the nonbelievers. How many chances were they to be given? Was Jesus's presence on earth, living among humans, to provide an answer or to show the way or even become the way not just for Jews but for all peoples? Was Jesus the solution to their negative actions toward God, a cure for their inability to follow the laws? His death was meaningful, for he did not die atoning for his sins but for our sins. Jesus committed no sins. We make the mistakes. Jesus served in our stead. The message from God is not exclusive but inclusive.

Used By God

Abraham was a wealthy man; so was his son, Isaac. Isaac's son Jacob did just fine, and his wealth grew too, despite family problems. David and Solomon were wealthy and had power. God used these people for his purposes, as he does everyone who will follow him. God did not discredit them for their power or wealth but looked to them for their willingness to follow and obey God and God's rules, to be an example to all. The poor too found comfort in the Lord and discovered their pain and suffering was tolerable when their faith was strong. We are all used by God in some way.

Just a few weeks ago, I was told, "Dad, you probably won't believe this, but next Sunday I am teaching a Sunday school class at church. It's about Noah and the flood." Well, I must candidly admit, I was taken aback and more than pleased. My daughter's two-year-olds were to be in that class, and she had an incentive and knew too how she had been encouraged to raise her children knowing the Lord. And she felt comfortable letting me know and knowing I would only support and encourage her to continue with such good works. She too is now being used by the Lord.

God Can Use You Too

God chooses people not because of their worthiness or because of favoritism. Those people in the Bible were chosen for the same reason God chooses people today: so that others may know him. In addition, many references in the Old Testament contrast God's fight with

Satan, God's intent to fulfill his plan (which is achieved in part with the birth of Christ), and how individuals should conduct themselves, lead their lives, and deal with their fellow man.

> *You are my witnesses, declares the Lord, and my servant whom I have chosen, so that you may know and believe me and understand that I am he. Before me no god was formed, nor will there be one after me. I, even I, am the Lord, and apart from me there is no savior.* Isaiah 43:10-11

Those chosen were not perfect people but *used by God* for his purpose. And being so used, they understood, as we can today, the power of the Lord. No matter what we do, we cannot be perfect in the eyes of the Lord, but we are being used. To be chosen by God means that God plans to reveal something about himself and his love through your life. I do pray I am doing what God wants me to do.

A Simple Request

There is a simple request. Believe. Just believe. Poor or wealthy, just believe. Strong or weak, just believe. In authority or not, just believe. And act accordingly. Be willing. Open your mind and heart to the Word and find your center, your purpose, and your calling. God has placed us here on earth for a reason, and the opportunity presented to all who believe is significant. Give God a chance. He can use you too.

God deals with the problems caused by man every day. It was a pagan world God sought to cleanse. He chose and worked with a constituency of faithful, and some less faithful, followers to succeed in his objective. Rules, laws were established, peoples were selected—individuals and groups—punishment was imparted, at times harsh and decisive, in an effort to make man more aware, knowledgeable, and able to share with others the inherent qualities of man that must shine forth and be engaged at all times to overcome the sin within, the selfish influences that surround us all and must be overcome to enable a safe, peaceful, caring, loving world community. This was of no avail until Jesus came to us as Immanuel, a God who became a man.

Use the time of Christmas as a reminder. Use Easter as a reminder. Use next Sunday in church as a reminder, a starting point if you are not already on the path, an awakening to make as your resolution for all your remaining years to come to bask in the light of the Lord and get to know him better through his Word and your heart. You too can be ever so thankful for what God and his Son have done for you and me and continue to do for you and me. God used his Son to save us from ourselves and the sins of mankind. If not Christmas, then Easter; choose one, choose both, but get started. You will then be used, and you will like it.

The message is to be thankful and to serve the Lord. Be loving and humble; find your gift and use it for the glory of the Lord. Work each day and do what you do not for yourself but for the Lord. Thus, you will be thankful for the life Jesus led, God's unselfish act of love for you by allowing his Son to serve our sentence and receive the punishment we deserved for the criminal acts we committed against God, and the way God created for us to follow.

What the Old Testament Reveals Historically

The earth is defiled by its people; they have disobeyed the laws, violated the statutes and broken the everlasting covenant. Isaiah 24:5

I take no pleasure in the death of the wicked, but rather that they turn from their ways and live. Ezekiel 33:11

History

Everyone goes to school. Our wonderful government wants everyone to have an education. Learning, understanding, and having the ability to utilize one's education for the good of others are admirable objectives. From first grade through high school and college, a subject taught every semester was history. There was

American history, the history of Europe, the history of the world, history of the Civil War, history of World War II, Alexander the Great, history of civilization from the Greeks to modern times. For most it was not a favorite topic and one that required remembering names and dates, people, and places. But history has value, and the value comes in what we learn from other people and their actions. Christian history is no exception. For me, it became the route to a location in my mind and heart where the Holy Spirit indeed was located.

An analogy to begin with is the game connect-the-dots. Page after page of a connect-the-dots workbook produce a vast array of images. Looking at the dots alone is as looking into a clear midnight sky and seeing a mass of stars. Until you know what to look for, such as Oberon or the Big or Small Dipper, it is just an amazing, beautiful view of glittering dots. Once you know where and what to look for, you can connect the dots and see various images in the sky. The same is true for the Old Testament; it is a series of dots on the map of Christian history. Connect the dots, and you will see the face of Jesus.

Unkept Promises

When we consider a relationship with God, we must think about promises. Take New Year's resolutions. We all seem to make them, or when asked what our New Year's resolution was or resolutions were, generally, even if we haven't made any or forgot to make one, we come up with something. With God, if we decide to make a commitment, then every day is a New Year, and every day we need to think about promises. Our commitment to God is making our resolutions. This is a big step. God already has established the promises he made to us; now it is up to us to fulfill our promises to God.

The Old Testament outlines God's promises, some fulfilled and some yet to be fulfilled. Then there are rules and regulations, which include the Ten Commandments. Try to follow all of them. Try to follow just some for a month, a week, or even a day. It may be impossible. A slip of the tongue, words not to be repeated when confronted by a driver making a wrong turn or neglecting to notice you alongside, the buzzer from God will be heard in your head. An exclamation or reaction to good news or bad news may elicit a remark that includes words you may discover afterward to be considered an affront to the Lord, especially if children are in the room. *Buzz.* Eat too much, drink too much, besides a few swear words now and then—*buzz.* Look longingly at a person of the opposite sex, even the same sex, and *buzz.* What are we to do? Do you desire your neighbor's new Porsche or boat and wish you could have something similar or better? Do you every now and then take time from work, call in sick, and really go shopping or spend a day at the spa or just sleep in? What about sick days? Have you always been sick on the sick days you have taken from work? I could go on with more examples. You can too. But what I am trying to demonstrate here is how difficult it is to live up to the standards God would like us to. I still find myself at times ready with a hand gesture when peeved at someone but must admit I am making every effort to keep that movement in tow. Golfing, which I enjoy, is an occasion to observe others and too often learn stories or hear comments or suggestions or again see the gestures and try to contain myself. Good people often say and do stupid things, and I am no exception. I have regrets from historical miscues left all over the place.

The Old Testament, if you get into it, speaks of the Jewish people—the leaders, the kings—who too often did not keep their promises to God, or they forgot. God just could not forgive them. How to live, what to do, are outlined in detail—Deuteronomy and Leviticus—along with historical examples. The life of Abraham, his son Isaac, Isaac's family and children, Jacob (Israel) and his twelve sons, Judah and Joseph among them, Moses's journey, the peoples freed from their oppression in Egypt (the Exodus), all provide—in fact, the entire Old Testament provides—stories, examples, and the foundational elements for the rules and laws documented in Scripture. From creation, Adam and Eve forward, the lives of those whom God chose help to lay the foundation for how man should dwell and live with each other on this earth. God made agreements with the people—covenants. And there were consequences for not obeying the most basic of laws. There are contained within the Old Testament many examples of God's vengeance and wrath—the punishment. The covenants from God to certain persons became the basis for the Jews' faith and the reason to obey God's requirements. They represent a basis for all believers.

God's Response

Even with all of that—a guidebook, historical testaments, covenants, the Ten Commandments, and examples of God's punishment—the people of the Old Testament continued to fail in keeping their promises, despite reminders. Just like those New Year's resolutions. The people of God, the Chosen Ones, did not believe as they should, and they were punished; their land was taken away from them. After King Solomon, only 20 percent of the kings of Israel and Judah followed God.

So if that proves anything, following God is not easy. In fact, it is most difficult. And God knew it.

God wanted to rid the world of pagan lifestyles and beliefs that placed man in the forefront; lifestyles that held man in higher esteem than God. Was it God's vengeance and wrath that made the Old Testament people unable or unwilling to defend themselves? Was it God's vengeance and wrath that caused their land to be overrun by outsiders? God took the actions necessary to free the world from its sinful proclivities. He did it to prove his point, to show everyone the meaning of his words, and to make examples for others to see and understand. God showed he was in charge. Does this sound at all like family relations or discipline at home or even at work? Mom and Dad instruct us in the ways we should live our lives and provide punishment or rebuke as necessary for when we err. "You're grounded!" "No more car for a month." "No, you cannot stay out past ten." "Call to let us know when you arrive." Are these expressions familiar?

One of our granddaughters has a list of things to

do before bedtime. "Complete homework, brush teeth, take a shower, get dressed for bed, arrange clothes for school tomorrow, set the alarm, say goodnight to your brother and sister, talk to God." There is another list for the morning, and it also includes "talk to God." Her mom is using this list to provide a guideline and implant healthy practices that will last a lifetime. I can't say I ever did this for our children, but I am certainly glad they are doing things like this for theirs. The purpose is to keep the devil at bay and to let the children know they are loved. God is still acting to have man make the right choice, fighting Satan every step of the way. God's vengeance was against Satan. God needs our help, just like our daughter and her daughter. God is using her to help.

One recent summer I played golf with a friend visiting for a few days. It was a Wednesday, and I had to do something earlier in the day for church. I would not consider this friend a man of faith, although he attends church, at least at holiday times. He is a good person, and no one would consider him evil. He was honest in business, successful, and fun to be around. He is loving and generous to his wife, even though politically they were of different parties and during their thirty years or so of marriage managed to cancel out each other's vote with each election. That takes patience, love, and goodness.

During our round, he inquired about my faith. He knew some of my history and allowed me to share some recent developments. It is a constant process. He then revealed to me his intentions prior to college to be a minister. Wow! He told me about growing up with others who had faith and were "religious." Curiosity overcame me, and I had to ask what happened. Well, there was college, girls, fun, and after college, success in business, a nice car, a home, a second home, travel, and more. Simply put, he informed me, "I found I was more interested in material things than God." I must admit I had to temper my desire to push him harder to return to his beliefs but thought it best to keep our conversation non-confrontational. I knew a door had been opened. Maybe God will cause a breeze to flow over him and rekindle his love for the Lord. He should know too, especially if he reads this, that my wife and I have him in our prayers—his wife too.

God's Purpose, God's Witnesses

God's purpose for choosing a people was to establish his presence, witnesses to his abilities, people who understood his desires and would be an example to others, and people who would carry out his plan. God is still working to this day to have his message understood, his plan revealed, his Word understood and spread, and his people to continue to multiply and grow in faith. Those who doubt God cannot know him or love him. There may be occasional doubts, small doubts, but not big doubts. He chose the Old Testament people and the writing of the Old Testament to inform the likes of you and me. He had us all in mind. He was scripting the "dots."

My biblical namesake, Thomas, had doubts. He had trouble with the thought of Jesus in a resurrected state, alive in form after pronounced dead following his execution, and wanted proof. "Unless I see the nail marks in his hands and put my finger where the nails were, and put my hand into his side, I will not believe it" (John 20:25). Jesus came before him and granted, "Peace be with you," and then he said to Thomas, "Put your finger here; see my hands. Reach out your hand and put it into my side. Stop doubting and believe" (John 20:27).

Do not believe in idols , golden calves, Baal, or anything else, and as God said many times and reported biblically, "I will let you live." Now that is a scary thought. Love cars and you die. Love your ski lodge and you die. Love your home and the furnishings and refurnishing opportunities and you die. Love to party and drink and you die. But this referenced death is a spiritual matter, and as with Adam, it is taking a bite of the wrong fruit that causes one to be separated from God. You need to desire a union with God and get some separation anxiety into your system. Eat, drink, and be merry. Enjoy life, but at the same time, do not make it your obsession; do it with God in mind. Make God your obsession.

Remember the fruit of thc Spirit. Think of lemons, juniper berries, peaches, pears, kiwi, guava, figs, grapes, and strawberries. A read of Galatians 5:31 reveals the answer to the riddle: Love, Joy, Peace, Patience, Kindness, Goodness, Faithfulness, Gentleness, Self-Control. With these words, I have been helped. I try to remember them before my actions or my words, thinking about the meaning, recalling the initial letters. It beats just taking a deep breath. With these words or letters in mind, my approach to everything seems more friendly and caring. Since I have jumped into the New Testament, I need to return to the Old.

Shiloh and Invaders

If we lower our guard against temptations, see them all as sweets to be consumed, we open ourselves to attack. Our bodies could be subject to gaining weight, disease or infection, obsessions and dependencies. With our defenses weakened, we may be subject to overthrow, to others, Satan, doing us harm. That is what occurred in Old Testament history. A lack of true belief caused the greatest treasure of the faithful—the ark of the covenant—to be destroyed or hidden, taken away from Shiloh "because of the wickedness of my people Israel … I spoke to you again and again, but you did not listen; I called you, but you did not answer" (Jeremiah 7:12-13). (The tabernacle with the ark remained or was removed to a safe place in Gibeon.) Our treasures can also be taken away if we are not careful, thoughtful, and faithful.

The "sub-prime" mess of 2008 destroyed many treasures. An example of lost treasures is apparent in the banking crisis which arose in 2008 and was caused by "sub-prime" loan problems. Loans were made at interest rates below the prime rate of lending of banks, to be reset at a future date at higher rates. It was a means to induce borrowers to borrow to buy real estate. Overly zealous banks, investments bankers, and independent lenders, at times in consort with government-backed lending agencies such as Freddie Mac and Fannie Mae, were willing to provide loans for homes on very attractive terms. Borrowers were more than anxious to accept no-money-down financing programs requiring no financial history to acquire. The government encouraged borrowing and aggressive lending in an effort to fulfill the American dream of home ownership for everyone, even those without credit, or the income to cover monthly mortgage payments, and in some cases to persons without jobs.

The attitude was that if a problem in making mortgage payments arose, the homes could be sold at higher values and everyone would be just fine financially. Our federal government is still trying to find the bottom to the decline in the value of the housing market engendered by the perfect storm created by combining elements of greed, speculation, and want. Financial losses across the entire spectrum of society have been substantial; many treasures of savings from years of hard work have been destroyed. The capital markets, the financial foundations of the United States, and world financial markets fell into disarray. There were many who were not careful, thoughtful, or faithful, neither objective nor realistic. Even the most skilled and knowledgeable in the government and the capital markets lost their focus and became part of the reason for a monumental reevaluation of the treasures of real estate and equity. Satan took control and proved what he is capable of doing. There were many invaders into the pocketbooks of capitalism and the results were bad. The net of blame covers everyone, and losses resulting have affected our entire universe.

The people of Israel in the period after King Solomon lost their focus too. Invaders with names like

Shishak, Tiglath-Pileser III, Sennacherib, Shalmaneser, Nebuchadnezzar, Antiochus IV, Romans, Pompeii, and others all found Israel and Judah easy pickings. Assyrians, Babylonians, Persians, and Egyptians all were invaders. The names are not as important. It is that people—collectively, man, focusing on self—then enable other men to take advantage. History tells the story of what happened to the people of the Old Testament who created their own world and economic crisis as a result of greed, passions, and other self-interests.

How did God feel about these changes and the attitudes of the leaders? History proves he did not like it one bit.

His people—many, so many—had failed God; they failed in obeying the laws, and did so so miserably that they were dispersed and the temple was destroyed. God left the city of Jerusalem, no longer to dwell among his people. (The book of Ezekiel provides more details.) But God would be with those Jews scattered by the many invaders and promised even to one day bring them back to Israel. Ezekiel 11:17 makes that point, especially for those who are his children, those who believe in him. God is always prepared to be with those who know him and believe in him.

God still cared for the believers. Just like today. The Old Testament people messed up, and God spread them around, destroyed things they loved, cherished, and coveted and made changes. He followed the dispersed people, as he follows every one of us, and planned for an event that would change everything.

Solomon

Solomon was the son of David, Israel's (undivided Israel) greatest king. David reigned from 1010 B.C. to 970 B.C., and Solomon reigned from 970 B.C. to 930 B.C. Solomon's mother was Bathsheba. It was claimed that Solomon was the wisest man who ever lived. He was very wealthy and had many wives, who influenced him. He failed to obey God but did repent later in his life. He wrote Ecclesiastes, the twenty-first book of the Old Testament. Ecclesiastes is a story, Solomon's story, that "life apart from God is a vain pursuit." However, even though he sinned, he was loved by God. In fact, when Solomon was born, he was named Jedidiah, meaning "loved by the Lord."[12]

Remember that loving God—even when you have doubts—and repenting and seeking God's favor with a sincere and honest heart are so important. It will enable some sliding, a few slips, even a fall, if done in weak moments and done so regrettably. It allows for repentance and a conscience that avoids repeating the same mistakes.

David

David, Solomon's father, Israel's greatest king, reigned forty years. We all remember David from the stories of David and Goliath. He felled the giant with a slingshot. He did love God with all his heart and soul. But he was not perfect or without sin. He made mistakes indeed; one was arranging the death of Uriah, husband of Bathsheba, by placing him at the front lines of battle where the "fighting is fiercest"[13] and asking the field commander to fall back from Uriah so he would "be struck down and die."[14] That was after he spotted Bathsheba, liked what he saw, summoned her, slept with her, and got her pregnant. After Uriah's death and Bathsheba's mourning period, David married Bathsheba. The baby who was then born died—revenge by God—and a new son was then conceived and born; that was Solomon.

Even though David sinned many times, he was quick to repent and confess his sins; he did so from the heart. He loved God yet was not a perfect person. His repentance was genuine, and seldom (if ever) did he repeat his sins. We are to learn from leaders like Solomon and David and hopefully not repeat the errors they made.

David is mentioned for a specific reason, and most of you probably know this already. But for emphasis: Jesus was born in the lineage of David. He would have had David's DNA . This is key; it puts the history presented in the Bible, the people we read about and learn from, in our pathway. We can learn and walk the walk they walked.

David's DNA

In the New Testament book of Matthew (1:1-17), the lineage of Jesus from his adoptive father, Joseph, is outlined. It starts with Abraham. David is about in the middle.

In the New Testament book of Luke (3:23-38), the writer (Luke) provides the family tree of his birth mother, Mary.

Both parents are clearly tied to David.

Jesus is doubly marked with the DNA of his parents and David.

The Bible tells all, explains everything, from Genesis and forward. Throughout, Christ is present, and our education of God's plan and promises is there for the study. The "dots" connect in making a picture of our Savior.

Failures of the People—Failures of Man

The Old Testament tells the story of failures by the Jewish people to obey the laws of God but more importantly, their failure to love God with all their hearts and souls. As much as God loved them, he did not expect them to be perfect; but he had extracted a promise, and that promise was too often left unfulfilled.

The aforementioned suggests the difficulty man has to obey laws. We too are all among those chosen by God, if we believe. It is not just the Jews. And we are at fault just as those provided as examples to us in the Old Testament.

To bring all of this discussion closer to home, in 2008, all Americans experienced the sub-prime mortgage crisis. For some, this crisis had a direct impact; for others, indirect. But for all, there was an awareness that greed in America had gotten out of hand. There was more than enough blame to go around. Everyone had his share, possibly some more than others. What is my point? "The ... crisis is all about wanting more than they can afford."[15] We share in the difficulty that *man* has to obey biblical laws, knowing for example that greed is one of the seven deadly sins. As Oliver Thomas said in his article in *USA Today*,[16] we identify with the "good guys." Biblically, that would be Abraham and Moses, not the Assyrians or Babylonians (Old Testament associations). And as to the New Testament, "We don't identify with the scribes and the Pharisees, and we certainly don't identify with those hated Romans. We identify with Peter, James, and John."[17] He suggests we are deceiving ourselves, not looking at who we really are. "Look beneath the surface, and much of what is plaguing the world is plaguing us. Maybe we're Rome."[18]

The Chosen, the Laws, the Failures, Believing

God loves the Jewish people and indeed claims them as his own, chosen for his purpose. Covenants were established and promises made. The laws provided clear examples of how to live one's life and how to conduct oneself. But a strict adherence to the law was not enough to be in God's good graces. Without a belief in God as an all-powerful, supreme being, there could not be salvation. Even before Abraham was marked by God, he believed in God. It was only after Abraham demonstrated his faithfulness that he was given a stamp of approval. Those who followed stamped themselves in the same fashion as an indication that they were in the family of those chosen. However, without belief, the stamp, the mark, the indicator was not a guarantee of a future in God's kingdom.

Too many transgressions by the Jews caused God to seek another way. In fact, the laws were impossible to adhere to, and one error, one mistake in satisfying any of the many laws, was a sin. And without forgiveness, all were sinners. God demonstrated in the Old Testament that an honest belief in him outweighed devotion to the laws and that when asking forgiveness with a truthful heart, one might be spared. A strict adherence to the laws caused moral dilemmas, as in the story of the Good Samaritan, and there was an imperfect solution if choosing wisely and compassionately resulted in disobeying the laws as written. David and Solomon were provided as examples of God's grace and his use of selected peoples and their gifts. But the chosen as a whole did not believe; even many who practiced, championed, and even oversaw the application of the laws were not true believers in God.

The Israelites were a people whom God lived among, his location in the temple, the place where God dwelled. An area of the temple was set aside for God, to be visited once each year by the high priest. It was a sacred place. Few ever entered. In one way it can be said the Jews were as a family thc body of the Lord dwelled within as today the Holy Spirit dwells within those who believe.

So it was that God living among his chosen people decided, after hundreds of years (the years after Solomon), overseeing his chosen people and their many locations, to seek a solution and provide a new avenue to understanding. This avenue would open his kingdom to all who believed. He wanted the Jews to believe and sought anew, the Old Testament providing all the necessary clues, to provide a clear and forecast means for salvation, and now not just for the Jews but for everyone, everyone who may indeed be sinners, as all were and all are. The Old Testament was proof of man as a sinner, never righteous, and always to be subject to God's wrath.

God's plan was to continue. His day that made the gift for all possible and Christmas possible (Easter too) was to come. The laws were obstacles difficult to jump over without failing, so a new path to salvation was provided. No man is righteous, not one, but as a believer in Jesus Christ, things change. And along came God's Son.

Along Comes God's Son

Thanks be to God for his indescribable gift. 2 Corinthians 9:15

Significant to my journey was getting to know Jesus, biblically and otherwise. The facts about Jesus's life are captivating.

Shared Power

At the time of Jesus (4 B.C.–31 C.E..), the temple, built by and for Herod, was not as sacred a place as it had been in prior centuries (especially in the time of King Solomon). It was a symbol of Herod's power, a temple for Herod (man's power) in part to gain the respect of the people, but Herod had his loyalties to the Romans because they granted him his power.

Power was then shared. The Romans were in total control with Herod as the head, Pontius Pilate as overseer, and the Pharisees, the Sanhedrin, and Sadducees.

The Romans wanted peace in the area and allowed for religious freedom. Let them believe as they like; just no disturbances. Factions were granted authority within the structure of government to maintain peace and stability. Overseers were in place and given power to keep people in line and to stop the troublemakers, even those who threatened their power.

Jesus was not a threat to Rome. But to the Jewish leaders—those in charge of the temple, the focal point for the Jews in the area—Jesus was gathering support, and they felt threatened, their authority in question. But was their concern perceived or real? To them it was real. They had influence and were respected or revered by many, and they could incite people to act, even if it was to their benefit and not to the benefit of the people as a whole.

Seeing Jesus or learning about actions taken by Jesus that influenced people or caused them to believe in Jesus awakened concerns by the local Jewish leaders. Right or wrong, the disturbance struck at the souls of the leaders, and they wanted it to stop. They needed to protect their influence, their control over the populace, their powerbase, for themselves and for the Romans. The Romans looked to the Jewish leaders (in exchange for their religious freedom) to maintain peace. The leaders felt that Jesus threatened the peace.

Representative of All the People

But Jesus was there for *all* people. He remains that way today. The leaders had become rigid in their focus on the laws, as written in the Old Testament. The history of the leadership over the Jewish people since Solomon—more than nine hundred years—did not reflect well on their true belief in God. Jesus, the Son of God, was there to help, to change their way of thinking. Was it obeying the laws that led to salvation? Or was it obeying God? Or was it impossible to achieve? God, through history, gave insight to the answer. But now his Son was needed, onsite and present in the area, to provide guidance and to serve as our substitute.

Remember two basic rules: 1.) Love God. 2.) Love your neighbor.

Be a good person. Be fair. Be honest. Be trustworthy. Believe. Jesus found the principal leaders hardheaded, entrenched in their own proclamations, resistant to suggestions, and blind to the truth. He discovered that they continued to disrespect the temple, using it to change money and to sell animals to be used in sacrifice. The leaders saw the sacrifice of a perfect animal as forgiveness of sins. But if people did not have a "perfect" animal, the temple leaders were happy to sell them one. It was a system that the leaders found as tempting to personal gains as their belief system. Believing was a matter of *doing*; do good works to honor God, and you would be rewarded. Jesus was there trying to tell them the system is not the goal; it was believing in God.

He was there to simplify matters, not just for the leaders, but for everyone. He did focus on the poor, the infirmed, the downtrodden, but his plan was for everyone. He avoided the big cities in his quest (except for Jerusalem), reaching out to his focus group. But his actions and many miracles caused rumors to spread, and in the few years (according to John) or shorter period (by the writers of the Synoptic Gospels), he became a household name. Controversial. Inspiring. Humble. A leader. A comforter. Filled with love, grace, and mercy. He let the people know that by believing they would find peace in themselves, with their neighbors, with their family and friends. And peace on earth. This is part of the Christmas, Easter, and everyday message. Jesus was preparing the people for what he was going to do for everyone and wanted them to see, hear, and understand.

As Christians, we need to renew our primary focus on Easter, since Easter is the day the transition for us all took place. We were transformed from having no chance to having redemption and salvation. Through Jesus's atonement, we were reconciled with God. Man was made right with God. "Christmas ... has now far outstripped Easter in popular culture as the real celebratory center of the Christian year—a move that completely reverses the New Testament's emphasis ... Easter, however, should be the center."[19]

The Kingdom on Earth

The kingdom on earth was being led by Caesar, and along came a man called Jesus, whom many called King. King of the Jews. King of the kingdom of God on earth. Was it his goal to make earth God's kingdom? For a short time or for all time? Believe and you will do good things, good works, as a result in believing. The more people who believe and become part of the body of Christ, the more a community of believers will enable this paradise on earth to become more like God's kingdom. We know all is well in heaven. It is on earth where help is needed. This is God's, Jesus's focus.

What God Wanted

With all that transpired over the years since Solomon and even since Moses, before the birth of Jesus, God's direct intervention was needed to make a point. But God's judgment of the Jews, as destructive and disruptive as it was, was not the last word. The house of David reigned over a united Israel—North and South were one. God desired that type of unity to continue, but leaders after David were not successful. With the birth of Christ, God's saving grace was a step toward restoring unification, but now included everyone—those chosen and all others. There was a New Covenant. God's expectations were to remain, yet fulfilled in another manner. Jesus set the example; he lived as a man among men to show how to live. He made disciples of others to carry his message and example, and he became the sacrificial lamb (a metaphor for the historical animal sacrifices required for forgiveness), not just for the sin or transgressions of one person, but for all. You are all included. This is why you hear the phrase so often, "Thanks be to the Lord."

What was different? What was new? What the Jewish leaders wanted and required was no longer necessary. The laws only proved how sinful the Jews were and how sinful all mankind is by the very nature of man. The example Jesus set showed the people what God wanted and the love he offered everyone. His disciples carried the message forward, and that message is noted for all to consider every year at Christmas, Easter, and every day. His disciples continue to spread the Word.

You too can be a disciple. To be one, though, you need to understand how this perfect person died on the cross for you and me. He was perfect; what crimes did he commit? He was sentenced to a horrific execution based on contrived crimes by people at that time. He died and atoned for those crimes. They were not his; no, not one. They were and are our crimes, our sinful nature, our refusal to obey, for which Jesus gave his life and for which we must be more than appreciative; we must be grateful and most thankful. This is the message we must share.

A Message for Everyone

The message of Jesus was not just for Jews but for everyone. All races, all genders, all nationalities, without regional boundaries, the poor and the wealthy, the meek and the powerful, the sick and the healthy were all part of his plan. His plan was all inclusive and remains so to this day. There have been many attempts to distort or limit Jesus's plan, some with great success, but the plan remains for all.

After all God has done—the many, many years prior, destroying the temple, displacing people, causing floods, droughts, fires, and famines, and so much more—it was not intended in any way to hide God's love. For God so loved the people. Yes, indeed, and what did he do? He allowed for his Son to be born and live among all people. He allowed his Son to die. That is simply an act that is almost impossible to comprehend, and yet it happened. But not an ordinary death; a death that led to a resurrection, a rebirth, to show everyone the strength of his love and the need to believe in God. And by believing, you know also and can be thankful for God allowing his Son to serve our sentence and make us righteous, which without God's love or his Son's sacrifice, is impossible.

Metaphorically it showed everyone (and still does to this day) the power of the Spirit, of faith, and believing in God. Jesus walked about anew in his new body for forty days, appearing before throngs, as many as five hundred at one time, to provide witnesses, to have the story be told.

Jesus's disciples walked with him before and after his death and resurrection to bear witness to his life, his miracles, and the actions he took in the name of his Father. They all doubted along the way but learned the truth and believed upon his resurrection.

Boot Camp

With Jesus, the bar was raised and lowered at the same time. It was lowered in that the laws became an obstacle too high to overcome, so Christ made it possible for all who accepted him to be part of his kingdom. It was raised by confronting man with the simple truth that man needs God, Jesus, and the Holy Spirit to succeed in his transformation. Man is a sinner. We commit crimes against the Lord regularly; our only way out is through Jesus, who saved us. The path to becoming a concerted, full-fledged follower of the Lord is a "boot-camp" experience. Basic training involves hard work, a focus on the objective of becoming a soldier for God, and having the sergeant harass, encourage, teach, plead, punish, and do everything in his power to complete the mission. This basic training is not a two-week exercise or a summer at Fort Wherever; it is an ongoing activity and a daily regimen. We all need to march to the commands of our Lord, accepting him first as our supreme leader, who would and did die for us.

What Others Believe

The order of the world reflects the order of the supreme mind governing it.[20]

In many religions there is a god. Jews, Muslims, and Christians have a God and believe in personal immortality. However, not all religions have a god, and the god of some may not be the God of truth. Pagans worshiped idols and called them their gods. I found it helpful, as you may also, to learn something about other major religions, non-Christian. It provided for me a point of reference, with some understanding of what others believe.

Buddhism

Buddhists believe in discovering self. Yet, Ravi Zacharias, himself born and raised in India, a country where Buddhism is prevalent makes the claim (from his book, *The End of Reason*), "Buddha denied the existence of individuality."[21]

And Marvin Olasky, in his discussion on Buddhism,

defines nirvana as, "*Nirvana*, the extinction of individuality and entrance into the cosmic all."[22]

Controlling the mind via meditation and positive thought is an important element. Individuals can become wise without the need for a god, who probably does not exist, in this religion. "Buddhism denies personhood."[23] It is a positive-thinking faith.

Olasky tells us, "The Buddha was born near the border of present-day India and Nepal and lived sometime in the fifth and sixth centuries B.C. (his followers disagree on dates)." [24] It appears to be somewhat of an anti-Hindu religion in its beginnings. Today there may be "350 million adherents"[25] throughout the world. It is the major religion in Japan and China.

Hinduism

Hinduism, the principal religion of India and Nepal, has many gods, even sacred cows. Persons are reborn into higher or lower orders depending on how they lived their previous lives. There is a supreme god, Brahman, and when smaller gods are worshiped, Hindus are actually worshiping and bowing to the supreme god. Karma is a path, and there are other paths to spiritual gain. Incarnation is a key element. According to Marvin Olasky, "The *Rig-Vega*, the earliest Hindu scripture, may have originated before 1000 B.C. but was not written down until about A.D. 1400, so some question its overall validity." [26] Hindu is the third largest religion with "900 million adherents"[27] in the world. Interestingly, there exist the "untouchables," those of the lowest caste in the Hindu system, of which there are "in India ... 240 million."[28]

Islam

Islam has attracted "probably one billion adherents, only 15 percent of them Arabs ..."[29] Islam welcomes all, without prejudice to ethnicity or skin color. Islam is also a monotheistic religion, governed by laws outlined in the Koran (Quran). Specified daily rituals are a component of the laws and the need for every Islamic faithful to accept and perform. Muslims are believers in Islam and also have a historical connection to the biblical Abraham, through his first son, Ishmael. Ishmael was born of Hagar, a servant of Abraham's family and the Egyptian handmaiden of his wife, who was encouraged by Abraham's barren wife (so she thought), Sarah, to have a child with Abraham to preserve Abraham's lineage.

> After domestic tensions developed between Sarah and Hagar, the Egyptian mother of Abraham's firstborn son, Ishmael, Abraham resolved the dispute by separating them ... Abraham sent Hagar and their infant, Ishmael, leaving them alone in a desolate valley. Muslim narratives locate this valley in present-day Mecca, in the western part of the Arabian Peninsula, about forty miles inland from the eastern coast of the Red Sea.[30]

The area became populated after that because there was a well at the location (a well in the desert was meaningful), and the city of Mecca developed around it as travelers discovered the site.

Resources provided by Dr. Egun Caner (a former Muslim, the first to become the head of an evangelical seminary) contrast Christianity and Islam, Jesus Christ versus Muhammed, Islamic works versus Christian grace, and other comparisons. The materials give us an interesting insight into Islam. For instance, in one of his outlines, he notes that Muslims do not know their eternal destiny (as Muhammed himself did not know), salvation is not guaranteed, sins are overlooked if the good outweighs the bad, Muhammed viewed men as superior to women, and God is impersonal.[31] These are in stark contrast to Christian beliefs. Dr. Caner offers many other differences as well.

Muhammad (born 570 C.E.. in the city of Mecca), the founder of Islam in about 610 C.E.., is in the line of Ishmael, born of one of the many tribes of Ishmael.

Arabs trace their ancestry to Ashmael, called *Ismail* in the Koran. The Koran, in contrast with the Bible, says that Ishmael, not Isaac, was a favorite son of Abraham.[32] This is a most interesting point in that it totally contradicts thc Bible and does so, as some have claimed, to substitute Ishmael for the promises Isaac inherited from God, and thus has no validity. Those promises are noted in Genesis 17:19-21. It is justification only for Muslims.

Muhammad was illiterate but came to possess the ideals of the Koran from the angel Gabriel, having it "cast… into Muhammad's heart." [33] As a prophet, he preached openly after a few years to a pagan Meccan society, and after thirteen years and an assassination attempt, he fled to Medina (the Prophet's City).

"Another ten years of battle ensued with the Meccans until the Prophet finally returned victorious."[34] There was no ill will.

Muslims do not pictorially represent the prophet Muhammad. In the Bible, John 14:16, Jesus promises his people "another Counselor to be with you forever." Some have noted that the Muslims cite this verse suggesting Muhammed as that "Counselor," clearly overlooking the follow-up verse, wherein the Holy Spirit is clearly that to which verse 16 refers.

Muhammad is reported to have been raised up to heaven, joined by the angel Gabriel, where he received his knowledge from Moses, the Islamic prayer. This was at the site of the current Dome of the Rock in Jerusalem. However, there is no evidence he ever physically visited Jerusalem, except by way of a dream. In that dream, Muhammad traveled instantaneously on a Buraq (a creature from heaven) from Mecca to Jerusalem. Even his wife, Aisha, possibly his favorite, insisted that it was not a physical journey; controversy continues within Islam as to a physical or spiritual visit. There are Jews and Christians who surmise that Muslims lay claim to Jerusalem only because the city is held sacred by those two religions—a "me-too" claim. For me, I will leave that to others to decide.

Muhammad's message was one of harmony, not the message we currently assume represents all Muslims today, a view of Islamic Fundamentalism.

Unfortunately, even though "Islam welcomes all," they lack, in my opinion, any tolerance whatsoever for those who leave for another faith. They have every right to defend their faith but not to suppress or preclude access to the information and foundations of other faiths. It appears they view their flock as incapable of discerning for themselves their path. But these are an intelligent people and certainly most capable of making their own decisions. Those who leave are infidels. Such infidels are subject to death. The possibility of death, subject to the operation of a "killing squad" that seeks out the infidels, is clearly present—a danger of conversion from Islam. Freedom of religion is not an aspiration of Islamic Fundamentalists. To quote Ravi Zacharias: "Isn't it ironic that when Islam is in a position of power, Islamic beliefs are forced on everyone." [35]

Judaism

"The worldwide Jewish population now numbers 13 to 18 million, with the largest concentration in North America (perhaps 5.8 million) and Israel (about 4.7 million)."[36] There is an ethnic connection with one particular people emphasized in Judaism, according to Olasky. It is a monotheistic religion governed by laws that, if adhered to, offer opportunities in the life everlasting. The laws are set forth in the Torah and the Old Testament—Leviticus and Deuteronomy. Jews claim heritage from the biblical Abraham, through his son Isaac, and subsequently Isaac's son Jacob, who was renamed Israel. Isaac was born after Ishmael, a child of Sarah, who was able to bear children later in life.

Israel and Jerusalem were the center of Jewish life. That is the case again today, although Jerusalem is now a shared city.

Mosaic Laws noted in the Old Testament dominate the lives of the Jewish faithful. Given to Moses, to include the Ten Commandments, God provided the guidelines for living. The laws are difficult to satisfy, and thus all Jews find it difficult not to be sinners. In the Old Testament days, the sacrifice of a "perfect" animal was to atone for failures to keep the laws. A "perfect" lamb was a most popular animal for sacrifice.

God became frustrated with the Jews, especially after Kings David and Solomon, as the chosen people failed to live up to the law and found their refuge in themselves, their personal needs and desires, in wonton idolatry. The Lord God was so infuriated with the people of Israel that he left the city of Jerusalem, the temple where he dwelled (Ezekiel 9-11, Ezekiel 11:22-23). The temple was destroyed. God did not return to be with his people until Jesus, and then God's presence with his people, those who believed, took another form. God never gave up but showed he was free to go where and with whom he pleased, providing a sanctuary for many Jews dispersed to many parts of the world during many years of invasion and occupation by other countries, other leaders, other peoples.

Christianity

The Christian faith numbers almost 2.2 billion worldwide. The Christians are also inheritors of the family of Abraham through his son Isaac, Isaac's son Jacob, and of his sons, but especially Judah and by way of the Jewish faithful. Jesus was born a Jew and raised in the religion of Judaism. Christians are accepting of people of all races. Of those religions mentioned—Judaism, Hinduism Buddhism, and Islam —only Jesus is believed in by Christians as their Savior. He came to earth and walked among us, taught us, showed us the way, and died for all people. He bled for his people. He could be heard, seen, and touched. God has made us understand the meaning of this great sacrifice. After he was crucified, he resurrected and appeared before hundreds of people.

Christian believers are those who accept Christ, his death on the cross, the reason for his death, and his resurrection. They are the ones in whom God and Christ dwell as the *Spirit*—the Holy Spirit. The Spirit is a gift. The gift of the Spirit comes through faith in Christ Jesus. According to Gordon D. Fee, a researcher on the Apostle Paul, "Faith is considered one of the evidences of the Spirit at work."[37]

Jesus was accepted by the Jewish faithful, those who knew well the Old Testament and the prophesies it contained. Many accepted Jesus readily.

Christians view God as a triune God—God the Father, Jesus the Son, and the Holy Spirit. "The Father initiates salvation, which the Son effects and the Spirit applies."[38] For Christians, "the Spirit marked the return of the lost presence of God."[39]

From the Old Testament to the New Testament, covenants were promised by God, but a new covenant was instituted when Christ became the ultimate sacrifice and freed the Jews from the law to simply believing, from works to faith. But more were included; not just the Jews, the Gentiles also, and in fact, all who believed. Christianity is unequivocally all inclusive. You too are loved by the triune God.

The purpose of the Mosaic Law—the laws outlined in the Old Testament—"was to show how impossible it is to measure up to God's standards by human effort."[40] As written and presented by God, the Mosaic Law was never intended to save. It was not salvation achieved by observing the law; certainly "proper observance ... was pleasing to God, but only as it reflected faith in Him."[41] The book of Romans provides much wisdom on having faith in Christ, a believer's justification, and the suffering of those who take heart in knowing the Lord. John MacArthur has written two volumes on the book of Romans, going in-depth and helping to make clear the message of the Apostle Paul; he is often quoted herein.

Sightings of Jesus after his resurrection were reported often and recorded soon thereafter. The timing of the recording of the life and miracles of Jesus lends itself to the reality and credibility of the faith and the individual. Much has been written about Jesus. The Jews and Muslims do not deny the existence of Jesus. He lived. He was a man on earth living and residing among others. His travels have been recorded and accepted. Both religions see him as a prophet but not as God or the Son of God; that is the belief and the reality for Christians. However, the evidence is compelling.

So many have studied Jesus's time on earth, location to location, and the sightings of both his miracles and his resurrection, confirming the events that took place. The evidence led to further exploration, research, discussion, and study, and with each stone overturned, the facts, the data, and the material gathered supported what Christians believe and what I do as well.

From the pen of Ravi Zacharias, "Only in Christianity

is the privilege given to believe or disbelieve without any enforcement."[42] Emphasis must be given the words *without any enforcement.* The "Christian religion is one of communion and relationships with the One who made us."[43]

"Jesus worked by changing the heart, not by legislating. Legislation can only force compliance. It can never produce the love necessary to change an attitude."[44]

I am free. I have freely chosen to be a Christian and to believe in Jesus Christ as my Lord and Savior. I pray all have the opportunity to be as free and to make their own choice.

There is a God—a Creator

I have set my rainbow in the clouds, and it will be the sign of the covenant between me and the earth. Genesis 9:13

With a focus now on Christianity, having some appreciation for other religions, we can turn toward making a connection with our hearts and minds. Salvation is important to understand. God's role in creation is essential. Man's freedom of choice needs clarification. The element of pain can be easier to deal with. And our role will be emphasized.

Sin and Salvation

Adam brought us sin by denying a command from God not to eat of the fruit of the tree of the knowledge of good and evil. Adam gave up what was perfect and sinned, in denial of God. He disobeyed God; that was the mistake he made, his transgression, his sin. Man's freedom to choose was now expanded. By disobeying God, man now knew more clearly the difference between good and bad. But God also gave his Son, Jesus, to save us all from sin.

> Just as the result of one trespass was condemnation for all men, so also the result of one act of righteousness was justification that brings life for all men. For just as through the disobedience of the one man the many were made sinners, so also through the obedience of one man the many will be made righteous. Romans 5:18-19

Once the life, death, and resurrection of Jesus are understood, we have a new beginning. We will understand the gift at Christmas. We will see more clearly and begin to focus on the prize that is Easter. This is another connect-the-dots sequence from Christmas to Easter. The Bible brings us to understand our potential for salvation. There are many, many "dots" presented in the Word, and when the connection is made, your heart will jump, you can imagine and will see; the "dots" will join in a way that is magical, inspirational; and the triune God will appear, not just as Christ, but built into the picture will be God the Father and the Holy Spirit. We simply need to open our minds and hearts to the sacrifice, our renewed freedom, and clarity will flow, faith will grow, good works will be done, and peace on earth will be made possible. Faith is a way of the heart. Faith is our connection to God.

Salvation, as the term implies, means to be saved, to be rescued. An older woman was about to walk across the street at a busy intersection. As she stepped off the curb, the traffic light changed. Oncoming traffic was more aware of the green signal than they were of the woman, but an observant and nearby gentleman immediately reached out and grabbed the woman by her arm. She was saved. She was most thankful as well, since cars began to speed by, a clear disaster should she have succeeded in her attempt to cross the street at that moment. Ads on TV show people walking past a high-rise as an effort is being made to lower a grand piano from an overhead window. The rope breaks when another passerby, seeing what is taking place, yells and then pushes the couple away. In that case, the word *fore* is the alert, a clear warning signal to anyone who knows golf, again saving those in danger.

For Christians, most see salvation as a saving act as well. We are being saved from bad habits, love for material things, sexual diversions, deviations or perversions, loving anything other than godly things; money is a vivid example. Placing idolatrous elements about the love of God requires change, a renewed moral thinking that is focused on what is right. Common is the thinking that when we die, we go to heaven.

If you consider the Lord's Prayer, the request is that "thy kingdom come … on earth … " Yes, here on earth, the here and now, "as it is in heaven … "[45] We are to be saved and be representatives for God presently, in our lifetimes, with a future also, to be sure. "Salvation, then, is not 'going to heaven' but 'being raised to life in God's new heaven and new earth.' We can enjoy it here and now."[46] This is powerful news, but it brings with it great responsibility.

From creation, man has been charged with caring for the world, looking after all that God made. Taking this responsibility seriously was another matter, since man digressed in taking care of man. Man first, world second. Who is first in your mind? Our salvation comes in knowing what took place on our behalf by Jesus, being thankful and repentant for what we have done (and will do) in defiance of God, and knowing that we are servants for the Lord, bodily in our human form as well as in our souls. In human form, we can work for God now, today, and every day until we die. We become stewards of the creation, newly created through Jesus's act of dying on the cross to save us from our sins, to stop us from jumping into traffic and avoiding the falling piano that would be sure to destroy. After our life on earth as representatives for our Savior, then God takes our soul and does with it as he pleases, depending on our service, our faith in God in the here and now. If we are then resurrected as Jesus was resurrected and as promised, we will then enjoy our new bodies, without blemish, without infirmities, without pain. We will enjoy life "on earth as in heaven" for eternity.

So it is not what can God do in and for us, but what can God do through us.

One last point and a comparative point to other noted religions: "Every religion except Christianity is man made and works centered, and for that reason, none of them can succeed in leading a person to God."[47]

Creation

God created a perfect world in an orderly manner. From a formless void, God created light, then the expanse of the sky, making morning and evening, then land, sea, and vegetation, then the sun, the moon, the stars, then birds and fish, and then animals. It was a rational approach and a well-planned product awaiting God's last gesture. Lastly, God made man in *our* image (Gen 1:26) and went on to say, "God created man in his own image, in the image of God he created him." (Gen 1:27) He prepared the way for man.

Something from Nothing

Can something come from nothing? As a child, I often looked to the sky with great bewilderment. How infinite it appeared. Where did it all come from? Where did it all go? Was there just a void, a vacuum, space without planets, stars, sun, nothing? And then why earth, a life-sustaining planet, in the middle of nowhere? How did I get so lucky to be here on earth as a human and not a dog, or chicken, or lion, elephant, or whatever? I could have been a plant. Just what is the probability for all this to happen? Here I am living on a planet hanging in infinite space, on a surface that supports life. It provides water, fruits and vegetables, meats, and air that sustains me. It provides resources that make living more comfortable and more interesting. And it all works together; each element on earth seems to need another. What is it? Well it is, I believe, God. He planned well, an intelligent designer. And he did this all for me; for man (and woman). There is no other place like it. No one has discovered, even though people keep trying, any place like it.

We are in Charge, Challenged

God even encouraged me and everyone on earth to delve into his creation. He put us in charge. "Be fruitful and increase in number, fill the earth and subdue it. Rule over ... [everything]"[48] How does it work? What are the laws that control nature? Why does it work so well? He challenged scientists to make discoveries, to learn about the earth and everything as part of man's role to *subdue and rule* over everything. Pause and consider, to date, those discoveries only reinforce the concept of an intelligent design of the place where we live. His challenges led to evolutionist theories, but they have not refuted anything that suggests other than our world was created from nothing. There is even the Big Bang theory. But as many have asked, "Who lit the match?" Even one of the more famous atheists, Antony Flew, commented on this theory of creation, "It is physically impossible to discover what, if anything caused the big bang."[49]

Scientists have discovered the "code" that makes a man a man and a woman a woman. Yes, DNA (and RNA). Scientists Watson and Crick were challenged and uncovered the formula, a code. It works for animals too. The code that is DNA is a mystery. Antony Flew recognizes the lack of a clear answer to the code, making note that its "very existence ... is a mystery."[50] The answer to the inquiry: *How long would it take to evolve such a code for man, for DNA, using Darwin's theory of evolution?* would suggest that even the existence of earth from the time of the Big Bang may not be enough time to evolve the code of man; it is so complex. Only God could have done that. Is there any other rational argument? The evidence is clear. Follow the evidence. "How easy it is to let preconceived theories shape the way we view evidence instead of letting the evidence shape our theories."[51] Antony Flew discovered his faith when he opened up to the evidence and realized that his years as an atheist focused on preconceptions were years of denial of the facts before him.

Free Will

God rested, and then with the world formed, the universe structured, all necessary support systems available to sustain life, God's creation, this perfect place designed for the man he created, man was given free will. Adam ate from the forbidden tree. It was his decision. And yes, the ability to make choices, the knowledge of right and wrong, was upon man. The preferred choice by God for man to make was God. But man could decide otherwise.

Adam knew it was not right to eat from the tree of right and wrong, the tree of the knowledge of good and evil. He knew this before he ate the apple (if it really was an apple) from the tree, offered to him by Eve. He knew this even before Eve was made from Adam's rib. After God put Adam in the garden of Eden, "to work it and take care of it,"[52] he commanded Adam, "You are free to eat from any tree in the garden, but you must not eat from the tree of the knowledge of good and evil…"[53] So Adam had the ability to choose even before he bit the apple. He knew what was possible and the outcome for disobeying God. He had free will, but

God, having put Adam/man in this perfect place and telling him what to do, expected man to follow God and obey God. Adam was free of sin at that time and could make choices.

Adam did not want to be alone. He needed a suitable[54] helper. God, from a rib he removed from Adam, created Eve. Thus, now Adam had a companion and someone to fulfill God's proclamation that man would be "fruitful and multiply." As the story goes, the serpent encouraged Eve to eat from the forbidden tree. She too knew not to eat from it; Adam must have told her. "The woman said to the serpent, 'We may eat from the trees in the garden,' but God did say, 'You must not eat from the tree that is in the middle of the garden, and you must not touch it …'"[55] So she also knew about the forbidden tree and the consequences, but the devil convinced her otherwise. "You will surely not die." In fact, "Your eyes will be opened, and you will be like God, knowing good and evil."[56] Eve then offered Adam the apple. He had a choice to make. He took a bite.

Free will can cause chaos. Once God chose to create human beings with free will, then it was up to the human beings, rather than God, as to whether there was sin. That's what free will means. In giving man the freedom to choose, God allowed for sin but provided a path to righteousness. Sin can cause pain. Mistakes made can cause pain. God allowed man to take chances.

Man must be provided opportunities to grow on his own, without a protective parent or society. Take the example of a parent, a child, and a bicycle. Training wheels or not, a parent at some point must let go of the seat and allow the child to ride the two-wheeler without assistance, even if a fall or a scraped knee may result. Success can result and most often does. But opportunities, chances, can also lead to failures, and failures can cause pain. But out of pain can come good. That good is a greater proximity to God, a better understanding of and appreciation for God. It provides an opportunity to get to know God better.

With free will also comes a willingness to accept God or not. Indeed, with all the evidence of the existence of Jesus, his crucifixion, and resurrection, man must know the reality of it all. However, man's natural tendency is to say no to God. Even with all the evidence, there is a refusal to accept the gospel, the good news, the word of God. Man attempts to avoid the gospel at all costs, but inherent in such avoidance is the knowledge of the contents and the power and understanding and acceptance the Word can have. It is because of what will happen to man. There will and would be changes. In simple terms, the impact on man's lifestyle would be enormous, and man is not willing to give up the material things of this world. For many, the human sacrifice for the spiritual gain is too much.

Even for some who consider themselves religious, they have religious systems. But these systems in their structure, in the disciplines they adopt, in modifications via interpretations to the Word or acquiescence to the secular world, they "attempt to escape the true God to discover or manufacture false gods of one's own liking."[57] The free will of men in many religious systems (Christian and non-Christian) is attempting to mask their unbelief, their humanness, in a justified environment. They find a place that makes them feel they are in God's world, under his protection, and in line to be saved by creating their own standards for righteousness, making what they do in their own minds okay with the Lord. They do so by redefining many of the clearly stated requirements of the Word for their benefit. That is not something man can do. As stated in Proverbs (30:5-6), "Every word of God is flawless ... do not add to his words." This was Moses's warning to the Israelites in Deuteronomy 4:2. Man does not "distort the word of God." (2 Corinthians 4:2)

Pain

There is much pain as well as joy in the human existence. Understanding the pain takes some doing. Pain can take on many forms: unexpected death, murder, hate, deviant behavior, normal death, crimes, and hurtful acts against man. Why? This is part of God's plan. The one thing we all must realize is that pain cannot be denied. It is part of life.

Think about the pain, the anguish, the ultimate sacrifice. God had his Son die a brutal death on the cross (and the events leading thereto), at a time when Jesus was just beginning, as many thought. How devastating for the apostles and so many others who loved the man who was Jesus. How difficult for Jesus's Father. There was a great deal of sorrow at that time, a great deal of pain and anguish, and questions arose. But what good came from this event, this painful occurrence, this sacrifice, this effort to quell the work Jesus was doing.

At the time Jesus was preaching, he was upsetting the political conditions of his time, impacting the control or power held by people at the time. They wanted him removed and quieted so their way of maintaining order would continue. It came to eliminating Jesus. He was an instigator, a rebel in their eyes. Was there justification? Was there good? Was their purpose served by killing Jesus?

Then there was Jesus's resurrection, and then there was so much more as people understood and came to know God and God's purpose. Christianity grew. From an area limited in size, from a man who traveled over a relatively small area, from witnesses to his death and witnesses to his life and his teachings and his miracles, grew a body of believers. From a few hundred people, to thousands, to millions, and today billions, good flourished as many came to have faith in the Lord. From great pain, the ultimate sacrifice, came great good. A succinct summation on the rationale of pain is provided by an authority and author on the subject of the resurrection, Bishop N. T. Wright, in his book, *Surprised by Hope*. "You don't get to share God's life and escape without wounds."[58]

Just for a believer to believe and express his faith can cause suffering and pain. We must be brave in upholding what we believe, as testified to by the Apostle Paul in Romans. "We rejoice in the hope of the glory of God. Not only so, but we also rejoice in our sufferings, because we know that suffering produces perseverance; perseverance, character; and character, hope" (Romans 5:2-4). Standing up to the elements and principles of his faith can subject the believer to untold anguish. Those who fear believers, who find their message an affront to their lifestyles, will make every attempt to eradicate the plague of doubt that the believers can bring upon their unbelieving constituency if allowed to proceed without restraint. Rome may indeed be preferred over ancient Israel. That is not a positive. We all need to fight the good fight and help overcome the evil in this world. If we want to be the good guys, then we must be the good guys and not just characterize ourselves as such.

As is the case in China and in many countries where Muslims are the majority and in countries with secular beliefs (Communism as an example) or where there is no God, where the leaders thwart the growth of Christianity, the leaders know the truth, and their suspicions are strong that such truth will have a negative impact on their control of their country. They fear that believers will erode their powerbase, their ability to control. By keeping many misinformed, in the dark as to the Word, suppressing the distribution of Bibles, maintaining a tight grip on Christian church services, spying on what is delivered from the pulpit, they think they will be able to maintain harmony and power. At the same time, instead they suppress many, disallow individual freedom, and for others they cater to material wants, attempting to provide satisfaction by ruling the personal self, the humanness, of the population they oversee. In those societies, we know there is emptiness, a need among many, a need for something more, not material, a need for a personal sense of satisfaction, a need for a feeling of goodness. That is found in accepting Christ. Those who seek God thus suffer greatly in such environments. They suffer every day. They remain under the thumb of a dominant, intolerant government or society, a society being controlled by the bad guys. Believers would love to emerge and shout about their faith. Those who shout, who openly profess their belief in Christ, may well die for their faith. That is pain; that is suffering.

Human Freedom

A world without human freedom "would be a world without humans ... Real love—our love of God and our love of each other—must involve a choice." God is all Knowing. "(God) has demonstrated how the very worst thing that has ever happened in the history of the world ended up resulting in the very best thing that has ever happened in the history of the world."[59] Deicide.

> The death of God himself on the cross. At the time, nobody saw how anything good could ever result from this tragedy. And yet, God foresaw that the result would be the opening of heaven to human beings. So the worst tragedy in history brought about the most glorious event in history. And if it happened there—if the ultimate evil can result in the ultimate good—it can happen elsewhere, even in our own individual lives.[60]

Yes, There is a God—a Creator

Yes, there is a God. The Christmas and Easter spirit embodies that God, his only begotten Son, and the Holy Spirit that dwells within. And God who is supreme is the triune God. As such, through the Spirit, God is embodied in every believer, and God welcomes those new to him and those who return and seeks their assistance in making our world the place that God desires.

God is a seeker, seeking all who will follow. "The only person who seeks God is the person who has responded positively to God's seeking him."[61]

"No one can come to me unless the Father who sent me draws him." (John 6:44)

Why Easter? The Resurrection

"The early Christians would never, never have made this up."[62]

As I was finding my way in the Christian faith, much of my research and reading focused on events that occurred in the Bible, the associated history and archaeological studies that gave credence to the location and time of the events. Everything seemed to fit, and without doubt, they happened. It is all so amazing. Locations of cities, temples, rivers, and mountains fit as described biblically. Stories about the Jews—their travels, their struggles—were also confirmed by writers outside those who wrote the Bible. Confirmation was assured that Jesus lived and traveled as described in Scripture. Then came the resurrection.

Easter is a wonderful Sunday, and the week before, Palm Sunday, always brings me back to my youth and the times I attended church with my mother and brother, dressed in our best clothes, hearing about Jesus entering the city of Jerusalem on a donkey, with people lining the streets, welcoming Jesus and tossing palm fronds. After the sermon, as we would leave the church, we were given two palm fronds intersecting, making a cross, a reminder of the week to come and the days leading up to Jesus's crucifixion. Everyone outside the church had the palm-frond cross and carried the item with respect and some insight as to history. I was, for some time, one of those Christmas and Easter church patrons, but it was Easter that was special, Palm Sunday too.

When I had children, the holidays were as special as ever. Attending church on a regular basis became a tradition as well for the family, the children, and as it turned out, for me too. Still, Palm Sunday was always a welcoming experience, to sit and hear the message of Christ, his journeys, his activities, his miracles, and his pending crucifixion. It was the lead-in to Easter and the resurrection. Did I believe then as I believe now? I really did not challenge the issue. I went through the liturgy and recited the creeds and the responses. It was rote.

As I read and studied the Bible and Christian history, this time of year took on such greater importance, more so than Christmas. The resurrection is at the heart of Christianity. Easter *is* the resurrection. It was a unique event, never prophesied as so many other activities of Jesus were. Upon further study and review, the facts indeed gave great credibility to the actuality of this world-altering happening. It changed me more at this time of my walk and discovery and growing faithfulness, more than prior. It awakened me to being part of something as never before happened and something that made all my understanding more than that; it made it real; it made Christ real; it made God real. As real as God was before, he was made more so once the resurrection clicked; yes, Jesus, having given his life for me, arose in all his glory to walk with man, not now as a human but as a body that could eat and drink and as a body that could walk through walls, as a body that could be transported. Jesus was doing what God could do and thus *was* God. Jesus was God made man, living a life of perfection, dying and atoning for my imperfect nature, paving the way for my salvation, and born again as God, man no longer. What glorious proof! Everything in Scripture was made whole, was made more than a book; it was the Word of God and a living document that gave me (and you) direct access.

Resurrection

The resurrection meant, and means, so much to me. Jesus died and then appeared again in bodily form. Wow! Those who doubted him during his life now saw him in the flesh; he dined with them, and he could walk through walls; and he was dead. Incredible! But real! Now I needed to know more.

Often debated, often discussed, foundational in the Christian faith, just what should you know about the resurrection of Jesus? A good read on this topic is the book *The Resurrection of the Son of God*, by N. T. Wright. In it he reviews the history of resurrection theories, in part summarized in the following paragraph.

The Jews, as God's chosen people, believed that at the end of time their bodies would be raised, bodily, from the dead.[63] You die, you wait, and then you are resurrected. Note that there is a waiting period in their belief. It was as if the Jews would return from the exile of death or metaphorically, from exile itself. Variations existed within Judaism. The Pharisees believed in it. The Sadducees did not. Others thought you died and remained dead, never to be resurrected; no subsequent event.

But Christians' belief (after death) has no waiting period. In resurrection, there is life after death, a life with God or with the devil. Heaven or hell, so to speak.

Purgatory

Catholics have a modification to man's outcome after death, depending on whether his sins are venal or mortal. So for Catholics, there may be a waiting period for those committing venal sins. The mortal sinners go directly to hell. For the venal sinners there is purgatory, a place for the final purification of those God has chosen or those who have not committed mortal sins, the Catholics' own waiting place, an interstitial space between hell and the alternative, with an opportunity to gain access to heaven. Once cleansed to the point of being holy enough, then access to heaven is possible. Through baptism and the sacrifice of penance, purgatory can be bypassed through God's grace and friendship.

Now I can understand the program but cannot find the basis for the Catholic approach biblically.[64] It is a program designed by men—religious men, well-intended and faithful servants—but still an interpretation. As far as I can determine, the word *purgatory* does not appear in the Bible, and it is Jesus, through his redeeming death on the cross, who "provided purification for sins ..."[65] There is no suggestion that Jesus did this in purgatory for others, but by his own life, death, and resurrection for all who believe. God knows the believers.

But I do respect Catholics and thank their religion for the early years of the Christian evolution and history. The Catholic Church has preserved much of what today constitutes the Protestant religions, has steadfastly kept the word of Jesus alive through the Dark Ages and the Reformation, and done much to instruct and direct their congregants to comprise a world that is well aware of right and wrong and the punishment for doing evil, living an evil life, or worshiping idols.

Still, its leaders, its popes, are men who are prone to sin, and their history demonstrates sins committed in the name of religion by the men of the church at the time applying personal, selfish, standards. They have done things that clearly God would not have approved of. Most recently, there have been many instances of priests abusing children. The sins were not committed by the church but by men, priests. Also, those men—priests, cardinals, bishops, whatever the level in the hierarchy—who protected those committing the crimes, claiming such protection was done for the sake of the church, also suffered in the guilt. They too committed sins. But sinning as a religious leader is not exclusive to Catholics. There are noted TV evangelists, mega-church leaders, small-church ministers, and all of us who have committed acts that God would deem unworthy. We are all man, and all man sins. And Jesus saves. There is no Mr. In-Between.

Early Christian Thinking

Anyway, something happened to engender the view of early Christians as to life after death, life in this resurrected form. So versus the Jewish view that all people would be raised at one time, the Christians had one: Jesus raised from the dead before everyone else. And they believed a total transformation of the physical body would occur.[66] The concept of resurrection changed. This is important; Christians believed their Savior, the Messiah, had been raised from the dead. The Jews of the time believed that when the Messiah came, he would never die, never need resurrection.

The resurrection of Jesus became central to Christian belief. "We have to conclude that something must have happened to bring 'resurrection' in from the periphery to the center, to the focal point."[67] This statement was from an atheist-turned-believer, Antony Flew. Prior to that event, resurrection was one of many components of the beliefs within Judaism. The Christian view is unanimous, as described by Mr. Flew. "The wide extent and unanimity of early Christian belief in resurrection forces us to say that something definitely happened way back early on, that had shaped and colored the whole early Christian movement."[68] He continues, "We have to say that the very early church really did believe that Jesus had been bodily raised from the dead. We have no evidence of any very early Christians who believed anything else."[69]

No Debate

One last point: Historians often debate resurrection and the timing of the writing of the four Gospels (Matthew, Mark, Luke, and John), theorizing or raising doubts as to the facts and the reality of certain events—those events reflecting the birth, life, death, and resurrection of Jesus. Historians do not debate the existence of Jesus—his divinity maybe, but not the fact he walked the earth and has had a great influence on billions. But the change that occurred in attitudes toward "resurrection" tells us so much, tells us more than writers or historians can possibly doubt. What engendered such a change in thinking and impacted multitudes was more than significant; it was and is incomprehensible, yet real. *It happened and made people believers*. It made the apostles go on to become martyrs, for the most part, in pursuing their acts of evangelism, telling the story of what actually took place, what happened to them that made them true believers. They doubted in the presence of Jesus when he was living, but upon seeing him in the resurrected state, so many of the statements he had made to them while alive and while they traveled with him, truths he told, became reality, became understood, and engendered their life-long faith in Jesus. The resurrection did it.

Paul's Conversion: Written Account—Timely

It is the resurrection that is the distinguishing characteristic of Christians. Historical evidence is compelling. Witnesses and written accounts close to the time of the event provide significant proof to the reality of the resurrection. Paul mentioned the resurrection and witnesses to the resurrected Christ in the Bible in 1 Corinthians 15:5-8.

Paul (formerly Saul) persecuted those who believed in and spoke of Jesus. A book I found particularly fascinating on the life of Paul, *Rabbi Paul*, by Bruce Chilton, offers much in understanding this man, this Pharisee who condemned and authorized the killing of people of the "Way," and experienced his enlightenment, his meeting with Christ, while en route to Damascus to meet in synagogues, sanctioned by the high priest (of the temple in Jerusalem), in search of more names of those to be condemned for what the Jews considered heresy. In 32 A.D., "Paul publicly took part in the execution of Stephen, a follower of Jesus, by stoning."[70]

"Stoning was laid down in the Torah as the punishment for blasphemy."[71]

"Steven's public claim of a vision came on top of a series of reported sightings of Jesus risen from the dead"[72] to include reports from Peter and hundreds of others.

Paul was on a path to Damascus to meet with other Jewish leaders seeking evidence of those "who belonged to the Way"[73] so he may take them as prisoners to Jerusalem. There he met Christ in visionary form but nevertheless real. "I am Jesus, whom you are persecuting,"[74] Paul was told. Paul was blinded and sapped of his strength for three days. Events led to Paul being used as God's "chosen instrument."[75] A disciple, Ananias, was sent to inform Paul of his conversion, to "see again and be filled with the Holy Spirit."[76] Then, before Paul ever met an apostle, any one of the twelve, he began to preach about Jesus and the resurrection. Jews even threatened to kill him, but he escaped. There were many skeptical of his conversion because of such a role reversal, at one time arguing against Christ and suddenly vociferously defending Christ as the Messiah. Paul's life up to this point had been as a servant of the Jewish faith, a dedicated scholar of the law, having studied with the most respected rabbinical teachers. And with one event, he converted.

> Remaining in Damascus (for Paul) would have produced only increased animosity. A return to Jerusalem immediately after his conversion was out of the question ... It would take years before he could enter Jerusalem again ... [He] departed for 'Arabia,' only returning to Jerusalem via Damascus three years later. The Arabian region—the country southeast of Israel, politically at that time the kingdom of the Nabateans—is where Paul worked out the implications of his vision for himself during three years of self-imposed exile from all the people he knew, whether in Jerusalem or Tarsus.[77]

Tarsus was Paul's hometown.

It was three years before Paul traveled to Jerusalem and met with the apostle Peter. There he confirmed what he had received and understood; he confirmed his belief in the risen Lord with a witness. Their notes agreed. Paul was in Arabia and had been preaching before Gentiles and Jews for years before encountering a witness to Jesus's life and resurrection, yet he related the same story, the realization he learned from time spent with Jesus.

> I want you to know brothers, that the gospel I preached is not something that man made up. I did not receive it from any man, nor was I taught it; rather, I received it by revelation from Jesus Christ. For you have heard of my previous way of life in Judaism, how intensely I persecuted the church of God and tried to destroy it. I was advancing in Judaism beyond many Jews of my own age and was extremely zealous for the traditions of my fathers. But when God, who set me apart from birth and called me by his grace, was pleased to reveal his Son to me so that I might preach him among the Gentiles, I did not consult any man, nor did I go up to Jerusalem to see those who were apostles before I was, but I went immediately into Arabia and later returned to Damascus. Then after three years, I went up to Jerusalem to get acquainted with Peter and stayed with him fifteen days... I assure you before God that what I am writing you is no lie.[78]

In Paul's letters, his most famous possibly the letter to the Romans, Paul speaks to Jews and Gentiles and shares the gospel, the good news that Christ died for our sins, he overcame sin and death, and thus, as believers we are "justified by faith." (This is the theme of Romans 4.) Paul always reminds his readers of their inclination to sin. He also struggled and fought the good fight his entire life. The nature of his authority as a converted Jew is expressed in his letter to the Philippians, while incarcerated in Rome. He had experienced all that a Jew possibly could, more than most if not all at that time, "circumcised on the eighth day, of the people of Israel, of the tribe of Benjamin, a Hebrew of Hebrews; in regard to the law, a Pharisee, as for zeal, persecuting the church, as for legalistic righteousness, faultless" (Philippians 3:5-6). It would be hard to find someone with more impeccable credentials. Yet he saw the light and became a disciple for Christ and for everyone by sharing his experience and his knowledge so others too could enjoy a Christian life.

Such evidence is difficult to refute and is most compelling. Documentation that led to the writings in the New Testament occurred within, including letters to the Romans, Paul's letter to the Philippians, and the account of Paul in Galatians, three to seventy or eighty years after the death and resurrection of Jesus. The proximity of the writings adds to the reality of the events. In comparison, it was over four hundred years before written accounts of the exploits of Alexander the Great became available. Everybody seems to accept the exploits and accomplishments of Alexander the Great. Historical, factual evidence, even documentation from witnesses of the life and times of other religious leaders from Muhammad to Buddha, to Joseph Smith, Jr. (founder of Mormonism) is lacking. Often too, background information, even archaeological evidence, of the prophets of other religions does not exist, and the writings are of the prophets themselves, not their followers. The supporting documentation tends to be one-sided, one-dimensional, without outside opinions, companions, witnesses to the person and the beliefs suggested. Christians did not make up what they believe; it has been analyzed, studied, debated, researched, dug up, and further analyzed as no other religion. The evidence continues to pour in as scholars and archaeologists continue to uncover additional support for the truth and reality of events that were the path to Christian belief. Many researchers continue in an effort to disprove what Christians already believe, but in their efforts only add to the plethora of supporting evidence.

A Christian Belief

The resurrection, as said before, is unique to the belief of Christians. If you study and find too that this event actually took place, was witnessed and documented soon thereafter, then you too will become a person who believes in Christ. Those who deny the resurrection are misguided. They may be good people, have spiritual elements, but they have missed or are not willing to embrace the evidence. For what it means, what it proves, is that the guidelines set forth in the Bible are indeed the word of God; the events in the life and death of Jesus and his purpose on earth took place, and everyone knows now the method and the means for personal salvation.

Witnesses to the resurrected Jesus were many, hundreds. God revealed himself to a few prior to Jesus's resurrection. Abraham saw God. Jacob wrestled with

God, and a few others. For forty days, however, Jesus appeared to many, providing visual proof. There are people today, most often atheists, who clamor for God to appear, to show himself as evidence. But that evidence has already been provided, and the historical evidence, the timeliness of the written accounts and the lives subsequently led by the disciples of Christ, people who died for their belief, add to the reality of the situation and the reality and deity of Christ Jesus.

As for the atheists, even if God were to appear to them, any one of them, they would doubt, they would not believe, they would provide or find an excuse for what they experienced. Certainly if one and not the other had such a meeting, it would be the other who would not believe, even if the atheist who saw God converted. God has appeared; God has spoken; hundreds have seen God, and a written account of those experiences exists. The encounters with the Lord should wake everyone up to the existence of the Lord and have everyone believe. What more proof is necessary?

> This is the great choice every human being has to make: Is the resurrection account true or only a myth? If the latter, it is an abomination, taking away any validity to the Christian claim. Believing that the resurrection was merely symbolic doesn't create liberal Christianity or a more enlightened version of our faith as many argue; it reduces Christianity to something utterly vain, a belief system like paganism. For if we were to believe Christ was not bodily raised, then Christianity would rest on the belief in a human sacrifice—offering an innocent man to die for our sins. This is not enlightened thinking; it is barbaric. It is

> why so-called liberal Christianity is untenable, no better than paganism.[79]

This was written by Chuck Colson, known mostly for his role in the Watergate scandal, the conspiracy to cover up the Watergate break-in, and the subsequent fall of President Richard Nixon. Colson converted to Christ before he went to prison. He is the founder of Prison Fellowship, the world's largest prison outreach.

Easter is the time of year that the resurrection took place. It is the day we remember and revere the life of Christ and his sacrifice and know too that God, Jesus Christ, and the Holy Spirit reign and are offered to everyone with compelling proof to believe, get to know, prepare together for the future, and as a community of the faithful, enjoy eternity—the day thy kingdom come on earth as it is in heaven.

To the Nonbelievers

Even with all the evidence, as compelling as it may be, the resurrection of Jesus Christ is denied, debated, or simply disregarded by many. Why? Well, it may be that they are afraid of the truth; it may be that they are in denial; it may be that they simply cannot comprehend what the evidence suggests and therefore ignore the facts. Such is the ignorance of atheists. They know the facts but seek every means possible to provide counter claims against, even when such claims are filled with holes and only serve to heighten their want not to believe. True too for Muslims, Communists, and other religious groups that do not believe. Even in the face of all the facts they cannot accept Christ as a resurrected servant of God, as a savior. Doing so would be in conflict with what they want to believe, not in what is indeed truth.

Why are there countries and/or religions that make every effort to suppress access to Christian teaching and the Bible? Why are Christian believers killed for their beliefs or attempts to share their faith in many areas of the world? What is so scary about a religion based on the love of God that compels non-Christian believers in some cultures, some countries, to harm Christians and to black out the truth as Christians see it or express it? Can they not trust their own beliefs to engender their own people to remain faithful? Are they not comfortable in the facts from their own prophets or religious leaders to stand alone, to stand against the face of Christ, to stand against the Word, the Bible? I guess not.

A Christian life is a difficult life. It is hard to follow the path presented by the triune God—no sin, a daily effort to avoid sin and to seek forgiveness and to forgive when sins are committed—and to work for the honor, glory, and peace of the Lord. It is hard for Christians too but is made easier by knowing God's love and support. But it is obviously harder for nonbelievers, even those who know the truth and choose to avoid the truth from guiding their lives. The example presented by Jesus as an objective for everyone to follow or be like is an obstacle of great height that to overcome requires great effort, much self-discipline, faith, hope, and humility. To many, the wall to climb is simply an objective they choose not to accomplish. They prefer the alternative. Maybe they need more time in boot camp.

Some Last Comments on Resurrection

Some final comments on resurrection, more on what it means than its actuality: I can only agree with N.T. Wright when he states, "Resurrection is the point where creation and judgment meet."[80] All people will rise from the dead. Jesus provided confirmation and evidence of the resurrection. When I say *all*, I mean *all*, and those to be judged, those who have done "evil," will be judged. For those who have done "good," they too will hear the voice of Christ and will enjoy the resurrection of life. This resurrection will occur on earth. We will be given new bodies, and "the purpose of this new body will be to rule wisely over God's new world."[81]

We have been given the gift of eternal salvation and life everlasting. Jesus appearing after being crucified provided confirmation of an innocent man's sacrifice, a Father's love for all his children, and validated the Word.

Wake Up; Wake Up—Open up to the Cross

If anyone would come after me, he must deny himself and take up his cross daily and follow me.[82]

The Gift That Keeps on Giving

Now this is something to wake up to, not just on Christmas, but every day. The gift is given daily. With a willingness to let go and let God, to have faith, every day you too can wake up to gifts. The gift is everlasting. It is truly the gift that keeps giving.

Believing is humbling. It is giving in to one's self and finding how to live, love, forgive, and discover God's grace. Our internal system can be aligned, can be made "right with God." You can be transformed by goodness and humility. From *The Imitation of Christ*, "The more you are at harmony with yourself and become inwardly simple, the more you will understand higher things without effort, for you will receive intellectual light from above."[83]

Your Gift

Everyone has abilities, talents, gifts that make them special, different, and unique. Some have gifts that make them wealthy beyond what they could have ever imagined. I do not see that as a mortal sin as the Catholic Church proclaimed in March 2008.[84] Actors, musicians, athletes, television personalities, successful writers, scholars, scientists, philosophers, among others, all have gifts, talents, and abilities; many have distinguished themselves and gained riches as a result. That certainly does not take away from the gifts, talents, abilities, and special skills of a teacher, a mother, a father, a healthcare worker, or any person whose career may not create immeasurable wealth or recognition. It is what you do with the wealth, gifts, talents, abilities, and special skills or unique qualities you have. And doing so in a way that is with regard for others, never considering what they do or who they are or what they make or how wealthy or poor they may be in any way that makes them lesser people.

Yes, it is easy to seek recognition or pound one's chest for one's success. Excessive celebration is a penalty in football. I think the fact it is a penalty is a good thing. Excessive celebration states well too on the problem, the lack of respect for others. It is a selfish claim of success above another. It may be hard to not want or seek recognition, but it needs to be tempered. How is it possible to be glad to be nothing? Think about it, though; that is the most humble posture. Advice from a past member of the clergy, Andrew Murray (1828-1917), a preacher and evangelist in the Dutch Reform Church of South Africa, taken from his book, *Humility*: "Seek not, ask not for exaltation. That is God's work."[85] Do not be proud of your gift, but be humble and thankful and continue to consider how you came about your personal gift. Why were you chosen for the gifts you have? How are you using your gifts for God? Or are you using them simply for yourself? "For we are God's workmanship, created in Christ Jesus to do good works, which God prepared in advance for us to do" (Ephesians 2:10).

God's Gift: the Cross

Your gift is what you are endowed with from birth. How you are motivated and how you apply those talents you have or develop is important. But God's gift to you is embodied in the cross. Marcus J. Borg is emphatic, from his book, *The Heart of Christianity*: "The cross is the single most universal symbol of Christianity in the New Testament, in Christian worship and practice, and in Western popular culture."[86] Jesus died a brutal death on a cross. God sacrificed his Son so we may live. God established a new covenant with mankind. For the law was given through Moses[87]; grace and truth came through Jesus Christ (John 1:17).

A side note of some importance: The Roman Empire was Jesus's executioner. It was the will of the local established authorities that Jesus die. Pontius Pilate, the local Roman authority figure, although questioning the guilt of Jesus, succumbed to the vocal demands of the religious authorities, and to maintain peace, allowed Jesus's crucifixion to proceed. Taking a basin of water, Pontius Pilate actually washed his hands of the decision, not wanting the blood of Jesus on his hands but on those who called Christ a troublemaker and a threat to their authority. According to Marcus J. Borg, "Christians participate in the only major religious tradition whose founder was executed by established authority."[88] Prior to being nailed to the cross, Jesus was brutally beaten and made to carry his cross to Golgotha, the site of the crucifixion.

The imagery is that pictured with Christ carrying a burden, the burden of those peoples of the Old Testament and all present and future mankind. You must add you and me to that burden. Christ carried our problems, our mistakes, our refusals, our sins, our bad thoughts, words, and deeds, our crimes, and our misdemeanors on that cross. The burden represented by the cross is man, our own personal burden that we need to bring to him, and by believing in him, we will find grace and salvation.

The New Covenant

The new covenant was "established by the sacrifice of Christ on the cross."[89] It is the New Testament, as contrasted with the Old Testament covenants, which were reflected in laws and works. The Old Testament offers some foresight into the advent of a new covenant. In Isaiah, written about 700-750 B.C., it reads, "He was pierced for our transgressions, he was crushed for our iniquities; the punishment that brought us peace was upon him, and by his wounds we are healed" (Isaiah 53:5). And in Jeremiah, 600 B.C.:

> The time is coming… when I will make a new covenant with the house of Israel and with the house of Judah. It will not be like the covenant I made with their forefathers when I took them by the hand to lead them out of Egypt, because they broke my covenant. Jeremiah 31:31-32

The covenant suggested would be new. "For it is by grace you have been saved, through faith—and this not from yourselves, it is the gift of God —not by works, so that no one can boast" (Ephesians 2:8-9).

Christ, during his last meal[90] with his twelve disciples, offered bread and wine, giving thanks while making a statement, providing a means by which to remember him always. The bread represented the body of Christ, his person, as food for all, to be fed by his Word and his sacrifice. The wine, representing the blood Christ shed for us, was a toast to the new covenant, made for not only the disciples but everyone. Christians participate in the Eucharist, Holy Communion, proclaiming their faith and to be reminded. They acknowledge their willingness to be judged by the Lord and proclaim a willingness not to sin, aware too that this may be impossible. It is the constant reminder that brings us closer and makes us more aware of church, the Word, and what we must do to properly maintain the gift we have been given. Respect the gift. Be thankful always.

God's Punishment Finds a Substitute

For the sins of man God needed to extract a penalty; there was to be punishment. The wrath of God was such punishment. Sin and you will be subject to God's laws, his judgment, justice, and resultant outcome. The penalty for sin is death. Writings in the Old Testament reflect often on the wrath of God, his vengeance, and his unrepentant dedication to making man stop sinning, having man change, and making man aware and knowledgeable as to God's punishment, what God's judgment was capable of causing—cities destroyed, the earth opening to swallow the sinner, consuming fire to eradicate those disobedient to God. Atonement for sins was possible. Forgiveness was possible. But man could not eliminate sin once committed. We are sinful beings. God's acts may have been extreme, but they clearly demonstrated what can happen. Wake up; wake up to God's justice. Perfect obedience and a sinless nature were God's expectation, but such is impossible for man. From *The Truth of the Cross*, "We have a duty to obey God because He has authority over us by virtue of having created us. That authority gives Him the right to impose obligations on us."[91]

To overcome this need for punishment God needed a substitute, a replacement for man and man's sinful nature. That substitute was Jesus. The cross, discussed at length by R. C. Sproul (*The Truth of the Cross)*, "displays the justice of God and the mercy of God."[92]

"Christ did his work on the cross to placate the wrath of God."[93]

God's wrath on the sins of man was on Jesus, who took on all of man's sins and took the punishment man deserved. The wrath exhibited in the Old Testament befell Jesus as man's, all men's, substitute. In the New Testament, we see more of the love of God, not that love was not present in the Old Testament, but more so in the New, as man now needed simply to have faith. Believe in the act of kindness, the act of salvation, Jesus provided for mankind. Look at the cross; see yourself in Jesus, not Christ-like, but sinful and lacking righteousness, being taken on as Jesus's burden, a man, God-man, who lived a perfect life, assuming at the cross all of our imperfections, all of our inabilities to deal with temptations, our succumbing too often to other idols such as money, self, and material things, and bearing the pain, the nails through hands and ankles, that were meant as punishment for you and me. 1 Thessalonians 1:10 says Jesus "rescues us from the coming wrath."

Jesus paid our debts for the sins we committed, commit, and will commit. He atoned for our sins, accepted the punishment that came—comes—from the bench of justice on high. Jesus lived as an example of a perfect person, never thinking thoughts other than godly thoughts, and he died for us, for us who have trouble getting through a day or even an hour or minute without being taken by our mind to forbidden places. We have been made righteous. "The point of the gospel is that the minute a person embraces Jesus Christ, all that Christ has done is applied to that person."[94] By embracing Jesus, I am simply saying you need to have faith; you need to believe. But the evidence is so compelling, the history of the events so well-recorded and documented, the witnesses so many, that you even have proof, proof enough to help erase the doubts and believe. Trust in God.

If you now have an idea, know the gift, or are willing to open your heart and your mind to the gift, then you will be born anew. It may be time, if you have not already done so, to open your heart to the Lord. Repent of your sins, your sinful nature, and allow God, the Lord, the Holy Spirit to become part of you. This occurred for me in a transitional way. The first time I accepted Christ, knowing and understanding what he did for me, it was more out of thanks. But soon after, I accepted and thanked him again and again, and so it continues.

So pick up your own cross and follow. As you believe, your burdens will become lighter, your walk will quicken, your pathway will widen, gates will open, and your eyes will see the new covenant.

"The apostle Paul wrote, 'Wake up, O sleeper, rise from the dead, and Christ will shine on you' (Ephesians 5:14). God says to the human race: 'Wake up. I need to tell you I love you.' Every once in a while people do wake up. When they do, what they wake up to is gratitude."[95]

"Thanks be to God for his indescribable gift" (2 Corinthians 9:15).

Many Roads, Same Destination

For the Lord, your God, will be with you wherever you go.[96]

God is who he says he is.
God can do what He says He can do.
I am who God says I am.
I can do all things through Christ.
God's word is alive and active in me.[97]

Church Welcomes

There are practices in many churches that can make it difficult for a visitor to feel included. The practices can involve the vestments worn by the clergy, the rituals taking place (liturgy) and sacraments (rites) that may be observed. Also, what the visitor wears can be a problem. *Must I always wear my Sunday best? Can I be in shorts? What is expected of the visitor?* In some churches, such practices of dress are customary to the public worship performed and required, or a tradition, of the religion. They can be quite formal, as is the case with the Catholic Mass. The priests wear distinguishing garb; they are clearly the leaders, the people who will mount the pulpits. In other religions, distinctive vestments are also used, some always, some occasionally, and some not at all. However, when I state "not at all," I refer to dress. But any worship service, regardless of its possible formal or casual nature, has a program, a liturgy, for that service. The program outlines the events that are to take place in the course of the one-hour or one-and-one-half-hour period established.

Liturgies

Church liturgies can be beautiful, profound, and engrossing but also confusing, exclusive, and intimidating. In the simplest form, a written program is provided the church attender telling when certain activities will occur, such as singing a specific hymn, reading Scripture, announcements, the sermon, and the benediction. The programs and the liturgy are the same. If not taught in Catholic methods or ideals, or Episcopalian, Lutheran, Methodist, Presbyterian, or other religious doctrinal ways, a church liturgy can make a new parishioner uncomfortable and feel out of the loop. And indeed they may be, especially when one needs to stand or sit, follow the crowd, or know responses to certain statements by the priest, minister, or preacher. In many churches, the responses are taught when teenagers attend catechism—classes teaching them the philosophy of their church and specific religion and the associated rituals. A liturgy may be a rote method for believing, being part of a church body. One religion may challenge another on its liturgy. And there are those churches viewed as non-liturgical. Events observed in the course of a worship service may be referred to as liturgical. What is the correct way to honor God?

A Common Goal

The Bible alone suggests sacraments (by interpretation) and provides guidelines or the means by which you can on your own meet and speak with God. You may have grown up in a given church or religion and just love the ceremony, the ritual, the liturgy. There is nothing wrong with that. In my own experience, the service was viewed as a solemn experience where, exercised in the house of God, showed respect and love. Also, there was a historical link, a reflection back to historical practices of the particular faith/religion. There are many forms of worship, from total silence, solemn chanting, traditional worship with old hymns, the reading of the gospel, the Collect, repeating the Nicene Creed, or the Lord's Prayer, to more liberal worship with drama, hip-hop songs of praise, and being able to provide responses to questions by the clergy, with and without notes, but the end result is the same. We all worship God, and for Christians, Jesus too. The paths taken may vary, but at the end we all see faith, believing in God, as the final goal.

Independent Believing

Jesus freed us all to believe and be guided independently by Scripture. Whether in suits, jeans, shorts, sandals, sneakers, Crocs, T-shirts, ties, or golf shirts, we can all receive a message. Same for our leaders; they too can dress the same and as comfortably as their audience. Must the leader be in papal dress? No. I must admit, I like to be clean, well-groomed, and neat, maybe not in a suit and tie, but sometimes. It is my own way of honoring the Lord. It makes me feel good. But is that necessary to have faith, to be receptive to the Lord of God, to hear the message of the day, to pray?

Interpretation

In many ways, religions of the world have made political fodder out of the birth of Jesus. They have created their own laws, their own how-to books of believing. They've instructed their clergy what to wear, what to say, how to worship, and how to celebrate, according to their interpretation of the Bible. But whether it is wine or water, bread or crackers, leavened or unleavened, a symbolic or real experience when partaking in the Eucharist, an essential sacrament, honoring Jesus, the end result is the same. You honor God. You are reminded of Jesus, his short time on earth and his impact, his message. You are reminded of the sacrifice, a body, an individual who died for the people, who shed his blood for the people and came back to life. Wow! And that sacrifice was made to forgive each and every one of us of sins, transgressions, acts against God.

Sacraments

As defined in the *Merriam-Webster Dictionary*, a sacrament is "a Christian rite [as baptism or the Eucharist] that is believed to have been ordained by Christ and that is held to be a means of divine grace or to be a sign or symbol of a spiritual reality."[98]

The root of the word is from Latin, *sacramentum*, meaning to "make sacred."

There exist different interpretations by men, laymen, and students of the Bible, Bible scholars even, of what the Bible may say and tell us to do in the act of worshiping and respecting God. But they all agree on believing in Jesus Christ, his life, his death, and his resurrection. They all agree as to the Ten Commandments. They all agree the Word is God breathed.

The Catholic Church details for its congregants and clergy seven sacraments: the Eucharist, baptism, anointing, penance, confirmation, marriage, and holy orders—sacraments of service. Other, mostly Protestant, denominations only affirm baptism and the Eucharist as sacraments.

A question that often arises among religions is, *Are the sacraments symbols or more than that?* Are they a means by which God communicates with the faithful? Are they a means for the faithful to praise God and give thanks? One thing they do is communicate, and they are a form of prayer. They are memorials, remembrances. Some religions regard the sacraments as ordinances, having been ordained by Christ to be permanently observed by the church, and these are principally the two: Eucharist (Holy Communion) and baptism. They still perform marriage ceremonies, anoint the sick, and ordain their clergy, but not necessarily as sacraments. It goes to one's interpretation of the Bible .

Essentials

Are the sacraments, liturgies, or vestments essential? The key is faith. The gift you are given is knowing and honoring God. The doors to believing are open to everyone. The path to believing is before you. The doors should never be closed, the path covered over, even slightly, by the practices of religions. The Bible is the door to the path that opens when you begin reading.

As one matures in his faith, sacraments, rituals, dress, the ceremonies become more relevant reminders, possibly a more solemn and respectful way to engage in his faith. Others may prefer a freeform way to do the same, to engage in their belief. The essential elements are faith, love, and believing and accepting that the Bible is "God breathed"[99] and your guide to further understanding and clarity.

All roads, should you choose and willingly believe, have the same end point, the light at the end—God. Some say the road is narrow, descriptive of the difficulty and need to apply oneself diligently to the effort to stay focused. It is not easy to be a believer; a sincere and dedicated effort is needed, but whatever the road, no matter how difficult, the result is worth it. The rewards are more significant than any of us can possibly imagine, a reward just to pass the driver's test, get behind the wheel, start the engine, and get on the road and stay on the road. Do not stray. Your final destination can be and will be the house of the Lord.

Clarification and Faith

If the happiness of a creature lies in self-surrender, no one can make that surrender but himself (though many can help him to make it), and he may refuse.[100]

Got Questions?

Given all of the aforementioned, you may be confused or need further clarification. If you need a guide or a support group, there are many choices available. Find the one with which you are most comfortable. But all you need is the Word, and that is found in the Bible. The end result should be the same for all.

A companion in faith is good. It can be your spouse (as it is mine, even though we do not always agree), a close friend, or a relative. My wife is a believer in the truest sense. Her answer to many questions is simply, "Believe; have faith." Yes, I agree with her, and I believe; but I need to explore, find affirmation, greater substance, feel the ground under my feet, research, read, find out what atheists think, what evolutionists think, listen to the Apologists, read about discoveries of locations referred to in the Bible, question statements in the Bible, and find answers. Am I a doubter? Well, after all, my name is Thomas. But no, I want to be able to help others, those who are not believers, understand, feel a greater presence of the reality of the Lord. I guess I want that for me too.

My wife has her Bible studies and reads a great deal. She finds comfort and support for her views, reinforcement in words by others sharing her faith. Everyone engaged in loving the Lord needs to continue to read and understand, question and review, ask and have questions answered, and grow with Christ. But they also must lead a life that makes others see in them a difference, a peacefulness, an aura that emanates from the body of those who believe. There is a countenance to those who believe, and they may not be preachers or clergy or wear their faith on a sleeve or make their belief that obvious; but there is in their presence a unique element, a special quality, an openness and receptiveness, an accepting nature that distinguishes them. They are not easily provoked or readily condemning; they are less judgmental and more open minded. They are not critics but find the good. They are not argumentative but prepared to defend their positions. They are examples to others. That's my wife.

Someone to share your feelings, express your concerns, explore the Bible, rely upon, to pray with, and to trust may be necessary in keeping you on your path, your quest to enhance, build upon, and develop your faith.

Open your heart, and you will hear God speak to you. Wake up to the glory of knowing God.

Faith

Faith is an interesting term. As defined by the *Merriam-Webster Dictionary*, faith includes a.) fidelity to one's promises, b.) something that is believed, especially with strong conviction; especially: a system of religious beliefs, c.) a firm belief in something for which there is no proof: complete trust, and of course, with a reference to religion d.) belief and trust in and loyalty to God. So from this one can readily conclude that faith can be a "blind" belief in something for which there is no proof. But then too, what if there is proof? How would proof change things? Would not proof be the simple confirmation of one's faith? Proof in the form of support for the historical facts, the archaeological evidence, the written documentation, and the timeliness of written materials, witnesses, as well as proof for the life, the actions, the travels, the instruction, the reprimands, and the reality of the leader, the prophet, the God? Proof will make the blind faithful see so much more, have greater confidence and conviction, and become a champion for their personal faith, belief in God, and in God's plan for mankind.

When discussing one's religious feelings with others, often in conversation where there may be some disagreement or debate, a term often put forth by one of the communicants is, "You just need to have faith. You need to let go." Another great expression along those lines is, "Let go, and let God." I like that one myself. But is that enough?

Think about the expression *blind faith. Just believe.* A strong conviction in something, someone, some leader, some idol, some issue, some political party, some agenda, some personal desire, yes, something. Many people have faith in something. And if we boil this down to a religious system, we have a focus on the faith about which I refer. But faith is just the beginning. There is a way to differentiate between faiths, I firmly declare, and that is via proof. Proof is the fulcrum upon which the balance bar is tilted toward one religion or, let's term it *faith*, versus another.

We have already discussed God, and my focus is on God, a faith in God; and without such a focus, faith may be that of believing in a something, even if that something is a feel-good, self-oriented, positive something. Buddhism may be in that category. Muslims have faith in Islam and its founder, Muhammad. Mormons have faith in the Book of Mormon and John Smith, Jr. Jews have faith in the laws of the Old Testament, the Pentateuch, and the Torah. Catholics have faith in the Vulgate Bible and the triune God. Protestants have faith in the Bible, without the chapters presented in the Catholic Vulgate version, and the triune God.

Catholics and Protestants are as one in effect, believing in God the Father, the Son, and the Holy Spirit, the triune God, but with differences in interpretation. Such is true to some extent within Protestant religions, interpretation, the "how to present the issues of the Bible" to their congregants, be it Methodist, Presbyterian, Baptist, Lutheran, Calvinism, Unitarian, or the like. Those differences I regard as political and hope some day all Christians are on the same page, the Bible as the central focus of Christian believers. But I separate from Christianity other faiths with proof. For the Jews there is also proof. But the Jews ignore the New Testament, a read they should attempt because in it they will find proof of the prophesies of the Old Testament, with the resurrection of Jesus as the tie that binds it all together.

Blind faith in a religion is okay as a starting point. Inherent in blind faith is doubt. With 2,000 years since the birth of Christ, 4,000–5,000 years since Eden, maybe 3,000 years since Abraham, 1,400 years since Muhammad, a few hundred years since John Smith, and so on, the history and the facts, cover many years, and many people question the facts. But evidence, as noted in other chapters, may or may not support the facts. What are the facts? Also, what are the doubts? Can the doubts be eliminated? Eliminate the doubts with proof. If you have faith, whatever it may be, think about your doubts.

Eraser Rule

Picture a large blackboard, a slate with chalk, available to write down each doubt you have. List them all. On the same ledge with the chalk is an eraser. List your doubts; include concerns and questions. Then do research, study, go beyond the text of the religion, and confirm the historical evidence. Go beyond the statements of the leaders, the teachers, and conduct your own study. Even look at the texts of opposing beliefs. Study history and the timing of written evidence and obtain background on the writers, both those close to the situation and removed. Seek answers to questions you have, and feel free to inquire even further. Listen to the Apologists for your faith. Be open to the Apologists for other faiths. Seek the truth. Explore your faith. As doubts are eliminated, grab the eraser and erase them from the blackboard. If new doubts arise, grab the chalk and add them to the blackboard. Apply the "eraser rule." Eliminate through study, exploration, digging, dialogue, research, and whatever means available, your doubts.

If the doubts remain or even increase, then your faith may remain "blind." But as you may start with one eye open, the objective is to end up with both eyes open, and open wide and wider. If that is not possible, the doubts persist; indeed, even that one open eye may close. But it is possible also that the one open eye may begin to see the light of another faith, and the doubts of that faith may be erasable.

But if the doubts persist and grow, then it's time to think about another avenue to pursue, and that avenue may be a new road, a new faith, a faith that you may even discover in your research and study, a faith that via the development of proof rids one of doubts, wipes the blackboard clean, and provides an open view to God. That God will be the triune God; I feel strongly about that.

Blind faith can be enlightened faith; can be a brightly illuminated faith. Each piece of evidence provided is as a floodlight switch being flicked on, the light shining on the truth, and as more evidence is uncovered, more floodlights beam forth; those floodlights clearly illuminate the truth, the faith. Proof is the beacon, the multitude of floodlights, the blackboard with few doubts remaining, the doubts erased; one's convictions will fall on the truth, a true faith, a faith in a real God, a trust in the triune God. Oddly enough, as the doubts are erased, the helping hand on you will be the Spirit of God filling your heart. Try it for yourself, and you will, I am confident, wipe your slate clean of doubt and be a companion believer with me.

I am a Christian. I have doubts. I have fewer doubts today than I had in past years. Each day another doubt is erased from my blackboard. Occasionally, a new doubt is added. But my faith is not blind, for I now see so much more, my eyes are open wider, and I believe more than ever in the reality, the direction, and just how much the triune God has done for me. I am hungry too, hungry to learn more, know more; my eraser in hand, prepared and ready to erase the remaining doubts on my blackboard. Most importantly, I know that God loves me. God has provided for me a great family, a home, food for our table, wonderful in-laws, fantastic grandchildren, churches that have been an inspiration, church leaders who have been caring and forthright, and so much more. There have been trials, obstacles, and tests of my faith. I have sinned. I have asked forgiveness. I have been forgiven. Each day I struggle with my humanness, but knowing how much I am loved by God, how much I am guided by the Word and my faith, and that God listens to my prayers, I find I am comforted. And that comfort is confirmed in the proof of God's existence, of his Son living and dying for all mankind, his Son bearing the burden of sin for all man, the ultimate sacrifice, the resurrection, and the Spirit that remains in the hearts of those who understand and that intercedes on our behalf. Those who believe in the triune God, who have faith, who have taken the time to study and have seen the truth illuminated, have a clean slate for a future in God's kingdom on earth.

So now we define *faith*, a belief and trust in and loyalty to the triune God; a firm belief, a complete trust in something for which there is proof. "Faith is being sure of what we hope for and certain of what we do not see" (Hebrews 11:1). There is proof; that we now know.

"True faith," according to John MacArthur, "involves the surrendering of one's sinful self to God for forgiveness and receiving Jesus Christ as Lord and Savior."[101]

Why Is Church Important?

Do not disappear from church and the pursuit of God.[102]

The Holiday Visit

Many people attend church services, especially at holiday times. Easter and Christmas are days that fill most churches with Catholics and Christians. They attend often as a matter of tradition. However, they do attend to be reminded of the birth and life of Jesus, his death and resurrection, and also to bc in the presence of God. The gift may be overlooked too often. Remember the gift. The death of Jesus was for the sins of man; he died so we may live. If the reminder works and the message takes on a greater importance, attending more often in the course of the year may ensue. The believer inside may get out. The protective cover on the seed of faith may burst and allow the flower, the love for God, to grow and bloom.

Can you be saved without going to church? Yes. There is salvation without attending church if you believe. But, and this is a big *but*, the church is foundational for Catholics and Protestants, all Christians. It is the container that holds the presence of Jesus for us all in our local communities, when we travel, wherever we attend. Jesus will be present, as will God. "Christ is the head of the church" (Ephesians 5:23). "He is the head of the body, the church..." (Colossians 1:18). The community that is the church is representative of our connection to God. Working together, believing, and praying together provides the communion, the reminder, the reinforcement, the support, and the knowledge that Jesus is a daily part of our lives. The church body—the members—constitutes an extension of your faith and provides an avenue to participate in one's faith actively.

Worship

With each passing day I find I look forward more and more to Sundays, the day my wife and I attend church. When away from home, we make every effort to locate a church to attend. The message takes on greater meaning every visit. It can for you too.

"One of the great longings of the human heart is to worship; yet, within that very disposition there are tugs in many directions that clearly contradict the essence of worship."[103] Worship provides a connection to God, to the Trinity. The Holy Spirit inside us moves us to a greater union with God. With a focus on the Lord, we intrinsically know the truth, and the guidance and comfort we may seek comes from the knowledge inside everyone. Through worship, our souls unite with the Lord, the Word of God, and our community. Through worship, our commitment to God increases, and our awareness is heightened, guiding us to do well, to do what is right in our relationships, activities, fellowship, and vocational pursuits.

Worship can become a daily occurrence. Daily devotions and the church and community of believers help to keep us connected, keep us bound to each other and to the Lord. "Worship is important because it brings each life into cohesiveness within itself and into harmony with others in community."[104]

"Worship is the submission of all of our nature to God."[105]

"In creating us, God created us to worship, and no degree of academic progress will ever replace that need."[106]

Worship aids in unifying the self with God; the church brings the self and community together for enlightenment, the exploration of ideas, guidance, understanding, and a unity of thought. Through its leaders, clarification of the Word is made available.

A song sung by Michael W. Smith on his album Worship Again, "Here I Am to Worship," provides some poignant words, a portion of which follows:

> Here I am to worship,
> Here I am to bow down,
> Here I am to say that
> You're my God.
> You're altogether lovely,

You're altogether worthy,
You're altogether wonderful to me.

Indeed, when you worship, you will find a loving God waiting to hear your heart speak to him.

Giving

There are so many ways to give to the church in time, talent, and treasure, and the rewards will be heartfelt. Each person has a gift, and discovering that gift and making that gift available to your community, to your church, will pay dividends beyond your imagination. Small groups, a Bible study at home or at another's home, can help you grow in faith. Helping at school, writing to your congressional representative to defend your faith, making others aware of your faith, asking others for guidance, insight, or how to become more connected, even to find a church, are all steps up the ladder to godly rewards. There are so many ways to open and/or widen the Way.

A Christian

A Christian is a Christian when he becomes part of a church body. "For where two or three come together in my name, there am I with them" (Matthew 18:20). This Bible passage suggests that a person alone is not the same or as strong in his faith as when with others in prayer or communion with the Lord. Being alone in worship is akin to golfing alone and making a hole in one. Yes, it happened, but without a witness or witnesses, it is difficult to record, except in your own mind. Same case applied to Jesus; his disciples were there to be witnesses to the actions of Jesus and to provide proof. That proof remains today; the Bible is the certificate of the proof of Jesus and God. And the church body continues to be witness to the proof.

The Teachers

Church leaders—the elders, pastors, priests, ministers, rectors, et al—have been educated in the Word. They are involved daily in the practice of their faith. They have knowledge and can make clear passages of the Bible, providing enlightened commentary. They are our teachers, making Christians even more Christian by strengthening us in our faith.

Romans 14 discusses the weak and the strong Christians, the weak needing the support of those stronger, more knowledgeable, more practiced. The leaders are students, scholars of the Bible and the history of the church. They know too the life and death and gift of God and Jesus and the Spirit and can instruct, lead, teach, guide, and console knowing what God would do and doing as Jesus would do to aid their constituency. They speak as Jesus would speak and symbolize Jesus and the church to their people.

This concept is foundational to Catholics. The church makes the Christian. Protestants see their priests or ministers as administrators of the Word but not as Jesus's substitutes, not on the same plane, but as memorial reminders of the gift.

Nevertheless, we need the church leaders. They serve the people, and they oversee the principal sacraments of the Eucharist and baptism; they guide as shepherds their flock. They take their responsibility seriously and should not deviate from the Word or attempt in any fashion to rewrite the Word to say or be interpreted any differently. "If anyone takes words away from this book… God will take away… his share of the tree of life" (Revelation 22:19). They are the teachers, as he was the teacher.

Join

Joining a church, becoming a part of a church body, is enlisting, becoming a part of the army for the Lord. You are joining forces to keep the flame of truth alive. You can be on the front lines, a part of the supply team, in reserve, in the mess hall, doing surveillance, in construction, building bridges; there are so many parts to the army, and you can find your role. It is a worthy fight, the fight for family, for life, for freedom to believe in the Bible, believe in what is good. To fight those who want to destroy the church, to fight those who prefer to do the devil's work, is fighting the good fight.

> Be strong in the Lord and in his mighty power. Put on the full armor of God so that you can take your stand against the devil's schemes… the belt of truth buckled around your waist… the breastplate of righteousness in place… your feet

> fitted with … readiness … from the gospel of peace … take up the shield of faith … the helmet of salvation … the sword of the Spirit. Ephesians 6:10-17

At The End

The end of days will come sooner than later if we allow the devil's children to overwhelm us all.

> Mark this: There will be terrible times in the last days. People will be lovers of themselves, lovers of money, boastful, proud, abusive, disobedient to their parents, ungrateful, unholy, without love, unforgiving, slanderous, without self-control, brutal, not lovers of the good, treacherous, rash, conceited, lovers of pleasure rather than lovers of God—having a form of godliness but denying its power. 2 Timothy 3:1-5

December's Reminder

Through the reminder in December, that day we celebrate the birth of Jesus, the head of the church, the Lord, God, because of Christmas, the world will survive. People who believe will prevail. The people of the world will awaken to their destiny. We are predestined, those who believe or want to believe or want to enhance their belief. Once touched by the Lord and drawn to him by faith, you have been chosen to become part of his family, an heir, one of God's children. And the children gather in their local churches.

Easter's Reminder

Easter is even more of a reminder than Christmas. It is the day of the risen Lord. Believers are joined in the future that God has in store for all. Through the resurrection of Christ, he has "enlisted us to act as his stewards in the project of creation."[107] The new creation has begun. Hope is in the air; we are surrounded by the love of God and his encouragement. A foundation has been laid for a renewed way of life in and for the world, so eloquently expressed by the author and bishop N.T. Wright: "What you do in the present will last into God's future."[108] Be thankful for what the Lord has given us all.

Even with tragedy, frustration, financial difficulties, and daily trials, I have so much to be thankful for. Thank you for a wonderful family, all loving, caring, good people. They are still finding their way, and we pray each day that the Lord will fill their hearts with the grace of the Father and the fellowship of the Holy Spirit. I give thanks for my wife, a loving, caring, patient woman, filled with the fruits of the Spirit, whose love falls in abundance on all our children as well as me. In addition, for our health and good fortune; there are so many blessings we have received that have more than overcome the dark hours, for which we need also be thankful. I personally have found strength in the Lord on more than one occasion as I found his hand holding mine, squeezing very tightly too, when I needed comfort, guidance, and an understanding of God's plan.

It is the love of the Lord and what he did for us on Easter that is at the very heart of every Christian and the foundation of my faith.

Let God Speak to You, and Speak to God through Prayer

We can recognize and become aware of God's existence just by perceiving the things around us.[109]

A believer is a more compassionate person. A believer, a person of faith, guided by Scripture, will be on the path to a more compassionate life, a more compassionate being.

There is a song, "I Can Only Imagine," sung by the group Mercy Me, and others I'm sure. Its words are telling.

> I can only imagine what it will be like when I walk by your side... what my eyes will see when your face is before me. I can only imagine. Surrounded by your glory, what will my heart feel? Will I dance for you, Jesus? Or in awe of you be still? Will I stand in your presence? Or to my knees will I fall? Will I sing Hallelujah? Will I be able to speak at all? I can only imagine.[110]

God is an awesome God. What will you do?

Your heart is your ear to God. Let him in, and he will talk and talk and talk. You may not be able to quiet him. He will be so thrilled to have found you as a welcoming receptacle for his glory. Just continue to listen. Be guided and obey the principles you have inherited. Let "Jesus Take the Wheel," another song made popular by the American Idol winner Carrie Underwood. A few words from that song, so clear to everyone; we have all found the road we travel filled with many obstacles; we have been scared and just wanted to throw our hands up in the air: "Jesus, take the wheel, take it from my hands, 'cause I can't do this on my own. I will let it go. So give me one more chance. Save me from this road I'm on. Jesus, take the wheel." That wheel is your heart.

And from Scripture we have:

> Make every effort to add to your faith goodness; and to goodness, knowledge; and to knowledge, self-control; and to self-control, perseverance; and to perseverance, godliness; and to godliness, brotherly kindness; and to brotherly kindness, love. For if you possess these qualities in increasing measure, they will keep you from being ineffective and unproductive in your knowledge of our Lord Jesus Christ. 2 Peter 1:5-8

Let his gift be your finest possession.

Once you have the gift, you too can be a disciple. You can share and give more than you will ever receive and do so willingly and unknowingly. You will be a torch-bearer for the Lord, carrying his light and showing the Way to others. That is what you can receive this Christmas and every Christmas. It is what you can receive this Easter and every Easter. It is available to you every day. Every day is Christmas and Easter in the Lord's house.

Will you understand him when he speaks? With an open and willing heart, you will gain more than you can conceive. You will be a vessel, a reservoir, empty at the start, but awaiting fulfillment, and you can control the flow. How quickly your container fills is up to you. Some have it half full and at times half empty, but getting beyond that juncture will continue to expand your universe, open your eyes, increase your awareness, and make you a person of God. You will enjoy the gift you receive and have it to share every day of your life.

Prayer

A recent sermon on the subject of prayer and faith caused a stir in the local church my wife and I were attending. It prompted me to consider the message and just how prayer impacts everyone, as well as how effective it may be.

Religion and prayer seem to go together. Images of Jews repeatedly nodding their heads against the Wailing Wall, a Bible or copy of the Torah in hand, reading, praying, and/or Muslims facing Mecca five times a day to pray, kneeling, bending over, their heads down near the ground, reciting verses and prayers, or pictures of hands pressed together, eyes and heads tilted toward the sky, are all indications of requests, thanks, acclamations, or more, of God. Blessings too, as if God himself were present. God bless you, bless their families, bless their friends, and bless those in need. We see athletes look above in thanks or questioning an unexpected or unwanted outcome, the question *why* expressed facially and/or with hand gestures. Even nonbelievers seem to pray or look to heaven for answers.

God loves his people. He wants to be intimate with them, have a relationship with them. Through the gift of prayer, there is the potential for that relationship. Friar Victor Hoagland, a Catholic priest and director of Passionist Press and member of St. Michael's community in Union, New Jersey, and contributor to Bread on the Waters,[111] writes:

> Prayer and praying are essential for your life of faith. Like breath to the human body, prayer makes the Spirit live. Without it, faith dies. On the other hand, a person who prays grows in spirit and life.

Also:

> God looks for intimacy with us. How strange that sounds! God, all-sufficient, all-powerful, all-knowing, wishes to draw close, to communicate, to speak to us, to seek our response, to hear our prayer. It may seem unbelievable, but it is true.

And more:

> Prayer . . . is God's gift to the strong and the weak, to the smallest child and frailest of the old. It's given to those who say, "I'm not really religious;

> prayer is beyond me." It's given to everyone, no matter who you are.

And lastly:

> By praying we fulfill the desire we have as human beings to know God. After all, we are made in God's image. Something in our being thirsts for intimacy with God. That thirst is described in the Psalms, O God, you are my God, for you I long. For you my soul is thirsting. Like a dry weary land without water ... so my soul longs for you, my God. Something in us cannot be satisfied unless we are drawn near to God.[112]

Prayer is an important tool for Christians. It is our conversation with God. What we ask for, what we seek, our thanks and/or praise he hears. But does God do as we ask? Does God heed our requests?

The church faithful had been praying for months for a young girl with terminal cancer. Let us call her Sarah. Sarah was an attractive, popular, caring, and active twenty-one-year-old young lady with aspirations for college and life thereafter. She had loving parents and had recently moved to a new community far from her coastal roots and friends. The family embraced the town and found comfort in a local Bible-based church. They made friends and became a part of the community. Sarah also found new friends and even a serious boyfriend. All was well until one day the big C found her, and her body began to fail. Once discovered, her doctors and oncologists began their practice of medicine, making every effort to rid Sarah of her cancer.

This fight took the course of many, many months, and progress was monitored. The family's new church became most involved as a compassionate body, wanting Sarah to be free of her illness and continue to live a life she was destined to lead. When the C seemed to be winning, weeks of daily prayer, even an all-night prayer vigil, took place. Visits were coordinated and conducted, and much love was poured out for the young woman. Unfortunately, she died. Her boyfriend even proposed to her, although the marriage was never consummated; but he let her know how much he loved her. All deaths are sad, and in this case, many were impacted by her passing.

It was the Sunday after Sarah's passing. Many learned of her death that day. The pastor, an articulate, knowledgeable, and gifted teacher whose weekly sermons were welcomed and well attended, skillfully began his message and during his discussion presentation, interjected his thoughts on Sarah's passing, knowing how hard the church body prayed for a different outcome. The message the congregation received, their interpretation, impression, or understanding, was virtually universal. They did not have enough faith to save Sarah. The pastor's reference was Matthew 17:20, a discussion between Jesus and his disciples over their failure to heal a boy with seizures and other maladies causing great suffering. Jesus proceeded to "rebuke the demon" and healed the boy. "Why couldn't we drive it out?" asked the disciples. Jesus replied, "Because you have so little faith. I tell you the truth, if you have faith as small as a mustard seed, you can say to this mountain, 'Move from here to there' and it will move. Nothing will be impossible for you" (Matthew 17:20).

The mustard seed argument to me suggested to the church congregation that they did not have the faith to heal, collectively or individually. How deflating! No one was being blamed for Sarah's death, but many felt they were being blamed for insufficient faith. Was this the bad news of the New Testament that accompanied the good news? This debate has no clear or easy answer, but I personally feel God's plan can be revealed; and prayer helps to make it clearer, whether a specific outcome is requested or via a tangential or peripheral result. We must know it is impossible to live up to God's standards; however, having faith in Christ, sincerely believing, is of great significance. Insufficient faith may be the conclusion for everyone; no one has it, and no one may attain it. But the Word leads us in the direction that one who accepts Jesus in his heart (and God knows who that may be) has faith and can be intimate with God. Transgressions may occur, but forgiveness will follow with repentance to those who are sincere in their faith.

As to Matthew 17:20 and the mustard-seed notation, may I share a personal observation? At the time of this event, Jesus was clearly alive; his death on the cross and resurrection came later. Although the disciples traveled with Jesus, heard his message, lessons, claims, and parables, observed miracles, and experienced his life, they had doubts. Those doubts impacted the magnitude of their faith. The disciples could never become complacent or self-sufficient in their belief; they needed constant reinforcement, as we all need. After Christ's death and resurrection, their faith and belief in Christ was much greater, and in fact, their lives changed; their ability to heal people, even raise them from the dead,[113], [114] was made evident and possible, but not without prayer. Taking Matthew 17:20 in context, the mustard-seed argument, along with Jesus's act of healing the boy, can be interpreted as another lesson to the disciples, another act of evidence of the deity of Jesus, and the reason to believe, and the need to believe what the disciples had heard and experienced.

As a slight diversion, let's look at Mark 9 and the parallel story of the healing of a demon-possessed boy. The companion Mark passages provide added insight. It tells a similar story (possibly the same story) but without the mustard-seed reference. However, in this paragraph, the father of the boy possessed, upon seeing Jesus and gaining his attention, told him, "I asked your disciples to drive out the spirit, but they could not" (Mark 9:18). Jesus expressed an air of frustration, noting, "O unbelieving generation," (Mark 9:19) and asked for the boy to be brought to him. The father then pleaded to Jesus, "If you can … " do anything to heal the boy, with Jesus's incredulous response, "If I can?" saying in effect, "What? Do you know who I am?" With the added emphasis, "*Everything* is possible for him who believes" (Mark 9:23). Jesus's question was directed at the father, whether he had the faith to believe in what Jesus was able to accomplish. The father's response (this is important and revealing), somewhat of a "Yes! I believe; however, I have doubts and need your help" by saying, "I do believe, help me overcome my unbelief" (Mark 9:24). Therein lies the rub—faith is never perfect. Faith and doubt, belief and non-belief are often in conflict.

Through prayer, we let God know we do not take our faith for granted. Faith in the triune God is not inherent in us as individuals, as Christians, but needs reinforcement and the constant reminder that Jesus, God, has the power. Through daily prayer, we continually renew our trust in Jesus, and the growing process is constant.

Can God's will be overcome by prayer? In Sarah's case, one might say her death was God's will—nothing could be done to prevent it. So why pray? When does God decide? Can it be last minute? If God decides last minute, is God considering all requests through prayer and then deciding his best course of action? Is God judging those who pray at the same time? God is in charge; thus, God is also in charge of his will. As such, God may be patient and make his will known as late as the time of the outcome. Prayer may provide food-for-thought issues to consider, the weight of believers bringing pressure on God, pressure from the faithful; even those who believe yet still have doubts but seek constantly to believe seek help from God to enhance their faith. But again, the results of prayer may differ from the individual or collective direct requests of those who pray. Those who pray are just petitioners. Like protesters carrying placards. The placards note demands, requests, make statements, express desired plans, or indicate positions to authorities, those they hope will listen and may even do something.

For instance, a person is dying of cancer. Many people pray, including the individual, to live. However, the person dies. The deceased's family provides comfort to those who prayed; a strong faith develops as a result. In this case, the outcome is clearly not that of those who petitioned the Lord. But the outcome had meaningful consequences. People of little faith became people with more faith or greater faith. The petitioners were heard, and the outcome was fruitful, productive, bringing more into the body of the faithful.

A similar example is one I personally experienced. A prayer group for a dying individual was formed consisting of nonbelievers, close friends of the individual, and believers, also close friends. A minister offered to be part of the group and visited the individual's home along with the friends to provide guidance and the Eucharist weekly. After over a month of this process, the individual died; the group knew beforehand that this was the most likely outcome and was told to expect such a result. However, what happened afterward was inspiring. Almost the entire group now attends church on a regular basis; many attend weekly Bible studies, and through this process, through a prayer for healing, salvation, and forgiveness, new believers were born, new people were saved, new people discovered the grace and love of the Lord Jesus Christ and God Almighty.

The Bible suggests that God does listen and can change. Faith or trust become an issue. For one group of the twelve tribes of Israel, those in the lineage of Reuben, they prayed for victory in battle, and their prayers were answered. Why? Because God knew they trusted in him (1 Chronicles 5:20). God told Moses he was going to leave the Israelites in the desert after they blatantly worshiped another idol, a calf made of gold. God said he would provide an angel instead to guide them. Moses could not accept this. He fell prone on the ground and prayed, asked God to alter his will. "How will anyone know that you were pleased with me and your people unless you go with us?" (Exodus

33:16). Moses's prayer changed God's position. People of the Bible have prayed for safe passage (Ezra 8:23), for mercy to keep evil at bay (Psalm 6:9), for no rain and then for rain (James 5:17), and more, and prayers were answered.

There is enough reference to prayer in the Word that it clearly suggests that God listens. And God can choose not to listen "if those praying are selfish, rebellious, a people loaded with guilt, a brood of evil doers" (Isaiah 1:4) and have no heart for God, as those of Sodom and Gomorrah. And we may not always pray aloud what we are really asking or even need words, as God knows our hearts and the Spirit intercedes in expressing our requests.

> In the same way the Spirit helps us in our weakness, we do not know what we ought to pray for, but the Spirit himself intercedes for us with a groan that words cannot express. And he who searches our hearts knows the mind of the Spirit, because the Spirit intercedes for the saints according with God's will. Romans 8:26-27

The term *saints* as referred to are *believers*.

When we pray, there are conditions:

- That if we ask anything according to his will, he hears us (1 John 5:14-15).
- If I have cherished sin in my heart, the Lord would not have listened (Psalm 66:18).
- He hears the prayers of the righteous (Proverbs 15:29).

- If you believe, you will receive what you ask for in prayer (Matthew 21:22).
- With thanksgiving, present your requests to God (Philippians 4:6).
- Be conscious of the Word of God, of his instruction (1 Peter 3:7).

The conditions do suggest that those who believe in the Lord and adhere to the Word, make every effort to lead a life without sin, and are thankful have a better chance of being heard by God. But Christ, God's Son, gave us new life and forgave us for transgressions, past, present, and future, so everyone's chances, knowing God listens to us all, of having our requests met, are very good. They just may not be met as asked. The element of faith is important, critical; believing thus becomes critical, a true desire to want to believe, asking help to believe, and God knows the heart, the truth of the heart of the believer, even the doubter. So go ahead; ask for the person, ask the Lord, petition, pray, to whom you truly believe.

There is a bottom line, however. The final decision is God's. "I will have mercy on whom I will have mercy, and I will have compassion on whom I will have compassion" (Exodus 33:19). Thus, mercy is the Lord's.

And indeed, the Lord spelled it out for us from Matthew 6:9.

> This, then, is how you should pray:
> Our Father in heaven,
> hallowed be your name,
> your kingdom come,
> your will be done

on earth as it is in heaven.
Give us this day our daily bread.
Forgive us our debts,
as we also have forgiven our debtors,
And lead us not into temptation,
but deliver us from the evil one.

When you cannot think of anything else, pray this, the Lord's Prayer, with sincerity and conviction. The Lord will hear all of your petitions, requests, and wants, seeing into your heart, knowing just what you ask.

So pray, pray, pray every day; never stop. Build your foundation in Christ; take him into your heart and allow the Spirit himself to assist you in your belief and non-belief so you too can become a skillful servant of the Lord. Erase the doubts of your non-belief and grow in the Word, the knowledge of God, and your discipleship will be clear to you and others.

Now You Know

When the kindness and love of God our Savior appeared, he saved us, not because of righteous things we had done, but because of his mercy. He saved us through the washing of rebirth and renewal by the Holy Spirit, whom he poured out generously through Jesus Christ our Savior, so that, having been justified by his grace, we might become heirs having the hope of eternal life. Titus 3:4-7

You now know the gift. It is all around you wherever you are. Know too that the gift will be there for you every day; you just need to look for it. But now you know where you can find it. The gift is part of you, in you, of you, above and below you, all around you. Open your heart and you open the gift.

What are you waiting for? Open your gift. Invite Jesus Christ into your personal life, your inner sanctum. Trust him.

Be thankful too. Another Christian song, "Worthy Is the Lamb:"

Thank you for the cross, Lord.
Thank you for the price you paid.
Bearing all my sin and shame in love you came
and gave amazing grace.

Thank you for this love, Lord.
Thank you for the nail-pierced hands.
Washed me in your cleansing flow. Now I know
your forgiveness and embrace.[115]

May God bless you. With love, merry Christmas, happy Easter, and may all your tomorrows be filled with the grace of God, the love of Jesus Christ, and the fellowship of the Holy Spirit.

A Christmas Prayer (by Robert Louis Stevenson, 1850-1894)

Oh God, our loving Father, help us rightly to remember the birth of Jesus, that we may share in the songs of the angels, the gladness of the shepherds, and the worship of the wise men. May the Christmas morning make us happy to be thy children and the Christmas evening bring us to our beds with grateful thoughts, forgiving and forgiven, for Jesus' sake. Amen.[116]

An Easter Prayer

What we need also is an Easter prayer. But you already have that when you thank the Lord each day for saving you from yourself. I see in him my salvation. Even though I continue to stumble, it has become easier to get up.

Here is my hand at an Easter Prayer:

Dear Lord, your sacrifice was so great and we, so sinful, are the beneficiaries. We could have never borne the pain, the suffering, and the punishment you endured for us. It was the penalty we deserved. May the Easter day make us remember your perfect life, your incomprehensible gift, and our need to take heed of our bad deeds, and rejoice once and for all in a new life with and for you, God, made possible to those who trust. Your love, oh God, revealed to us by your Son, Christ, and made manifest in his resurrection and the Holy Spirit that dwells in the heart of the believer, transcends all other love. Your grace and glory along with the promise of an eternal life in your presence is more than we can ever fully understand. We accept it with gratitude and thanksgiving. You are our hope. Thanks be to God. Amen.

Finding Your Footing

. . . the mind controlled by the Spirit is life and peace. The sinful mind is hostile to God. It does not submit to God's law, nor can it do so. Those controlled by the sinful nature cannot please God.

Romans 8:6-8

Since I have basically finished my testimony and hopefully you have found something in this for you, if you are one of the 80 percent of Americans who believe there is a higher power, a supreme being, a God, then you might want to think about your future. There are steps you can take to make yourself a stronger, deeper believer. If the Spirit is not already moving you in the direction you want, there are steps you can take. To rediscover a faith you once had and would like to renew, there are steps you can take. To find a new focus, a new life, the excitement, the thrill of getting to know God on a more personal basis, there are steps you can take, as I am doing, and as I have written in this book. To make a budding faith a stronger faith, there are steps you can take. There are steps you can take to enable you to be a defender of your faith.

Finding Your Footing

First, you must know it will not be easy. In fact, it will be as hard as anything you have ever done—harder. Know, however, it will be the most rewarding thing you have ever done. Eternal life with the Supreme Being, the triune God, will be a reward. The alternative is not a very good one, and even if we never do meet God's standards, it is worth the effort. If you truly believe, he will be waiting for you. If you decide to do something, to increase your knowledge, your understanding, your faith, you do so voluntarily. You will not be coerced. You can raise questions, issues, and concerns and still believe and be secure. Just open yourself up to trusting the Lord. Save yourself from the condemnation you deserve, I deserve, for the many transgressions we have committed. Christ assumed your position, took your sins and the punishment we deserved, and died so we may live. Have faith. Do not be afraid. Take the first step if you haven't already.

As a Christian, you will not be threatened, at least not by another truly believing Christian, should you take a different path. Should you find a different path, others will pray for you; they will pray that you return to your faith, to the open arms of the loving God. They will be waiting to help you in your return should that be necessary.

I am not a perfect person. I sin; yes, probably every day. As one who believes, I am more conscious of when I am doing wrong or have done wrong. When I was young and single, yes, I did bad things. Drinking, women, sarcasm, good times, selfish, thoughtless acts, the usual. I have done my share of hurting others, even ones I have loved. Now I ask forgiveness every day. Each day I pray the Lord will give me the strength to maintain my momentum, to be mindful of my actions and aware of my frailty and sinful nature so that I may be more able to contend with my struggle as God intended. Every day I also provide thanks, thanks for the sunshine, the needed rain, the flowers, the mountains, the air we breathe, the beauty of people, the challenges that make me a better person, fellowships, and the ups and downs of life that make me humble. It has not been a smooth life; I have suffered, and I have been rewarded. It all takes acceptance, courage, and thanks. I thank God for giving me the inspiration to write this book, if not just for a means for me to get closer to the Lord.

We are passing through this life to make it to another. The trials we face daily only prepare us and make us eligible for being a part of God's sanctuary. Our purpose in life, according to Rick Warren, author of *The Purpose Driven Life*, has a starting point and that is with "God and his eternal plan for each life. Real meaning comes from understanding God's purpose for putting us on earth." There is, however, a battle going on. To fight the battle, more recruits are needed; more people must help by joining the Christian army and discipleship for Christ. We need more soldiers to help put on the armor of the triune God and fight the efforts of those who do not believe so that the world will become a better place. We are not fighting to kill those who do not have faith but to love them into understanding that through their free will they can find God and live in the light, avoiding the darkness, and make their home, their surroundings, their state, and their country a safe and welcoming place, for all mankind.

We all can do more. We can do more just as believers, having faith and making others aware of our values and beliefs. They will see in us a change for the good, and such a change can be infectious. It is the infection, an epidemic of believers, of those who find the love of God a powerful incentive to do good and have hope that can change the world. This infection needs to spread.

I'd like to believe that by this writing I have started an epidemic of believers, people, laymen like me, willing to dig deeper into the Word and into their hearts to help in eternal encouragement and to give strength for good deeds and words.

Walk With Me

I have taken you along my road and my path, leading me to a close association with the triune God. The Holy Spirit was my driver. I continue my trek, at times a hike, at times a walk, and at times a run, making my relationship with the Lord more exciting with every day that passes and every passage I reread. The run at times is when I see more clearly the face of God and want to get as close to him as possible that much sooner. There have been doubts at times that have slowed me down and interrupted my run—obstacles—but I am working on those doubts, making the effort, out of pure desire and faith, to overcome the obstacles. Each step is a step of thanks.

Writing this book has been for me my epiphany, from a thoughtful consideration of Christ as my savior, to a conviction and more knowledgeable awareness of the fact that my Savior lives. I have been enabled as never before to share my faith. Come walk with me, and if you feel more energetic, run with me. God will be alongside. Together we can *wake up* the world to a faith in Jesus Christ. The benefits are not just in personal salvation, but saving the world as a whole by returning to a popular culture that emphasizes the highest of moral standards.

The whole reason for being saved now is to be able to have an essential purpose in life. If we want our children to grow up in a world different from what we are experiencing today, we need to start making it different now. Our children will reflect what we are, how we live, and what we believe. "Know that the Lord is God, it is he who made us, and we are his" (Psalm 100:3).

Thanks be to God.

May the love of our Lord Jesus Christ, the grace of God the Father, and the fellowship of the Holy Spirit be with you.

Endnotes

1. *The Story of Christianity, Volume 1* (1984), *Volume 2* (1985), Justo L. Gonzalez, Harper,San Francisco, CA.
2. An excerpt from *The Night Before Christmas* by Clement C. Moore orig. written in 1822, The Heirloom Edition, Running Press, Philadelphia, PA 2001.
3. And may I recommend Kringle from a bakery in Wisconsin. Here's the address. I prefer the almond paste. Bendtsen's Bakery, 3200 Washington Avenue, Racine, WI 53405.
4. *The Imitation of Christ*, author Thomas a'Klempis, rewritten and updated by Harold J. Chadwick, publisher Bridge-Logos, Orlando, FL. Copyright 1999. Orig. written 1427. page 120.
5. The Holy Bible, NIV, 2 Timothy 3:16. "*All Scripture is God -breathed and it is useful for teaching, rebuking, correcting and training in righteousness, so that the man of God may be equipped for every good work.*"

6. *The God Delusion*, Richard Dawkins, pg. 343, 2006, Bantam Press, Great Britain

7. *The Truth of the Cross*, R. C. Sproul, pg. 164, Reformation Trust Publishing, Orlando, FL, 2007

8. Quote of John Adams taken from *The Politically Incorrect Guide to the Bible* , by Robert J. Hutchinson, 2007, Regnery Publishing, Inc. , Washington, DC. Page 181

9. *Surprised by Hope*, by N. T. Wright. HarperCollins and HarperOne, New York, NY. 2008. Pg.228.

10. *Surprised by Hope*, by N. T. Wright. HarperCollins and HarperOne, New York, NY. 2008. Pg.221

11. *The Problem of Pain*, C. S. Lewis. 1940, restored 1996. pub. HarperSanFrancisco, San Francisco, CA. Pages 106-107

12. *The* NIV *Study Bible*, Zondervan, Grand Rapids, MI, 1985, footnote "g" to 2 Samuel 12:25, pg. 440

13. 2 Samuel 11:15, NIV Bible

14. 2 Samuel 11:15, NIV Bible

15. Ungodly Hubris, an article by Oliver Thomas, *USA Today*, Monday, October 27, 2008, page 15A

16. Ungodly Hubris, an article by Oliver Thomas, *USA Today*, Monday, October 27, 2008, page 15A

17. Ungodly Hubris, an article by Oliver Thomas, *USA Today*, Monday, October 27, 2008, page 15A

18. Ungodly Hubris, an article by Oliver Thomas, *USA Today*, Monday, October 27, 2008, page 15A

19. *Surprised by Hope*, N. T. Wright, HarperCollins Publishers, New York, NY, 2008, pg.23

20. Quote of Palle Yourgrau taken from *There is A God – How the World's Most Notorious Atheist Changed His Mind*, by Antony Flew with Roy Abraham Varghese, 2007, published by HarperOne Page 167

21. *The End of Reason,* by Ravi Zacharias. Zondervan Publishing, Grand Rapids, MI. 2008. Pg. 91

22. *The Religions Next Door*, by Marvin Olasky, Broadman and Holman Publishers, Nashville, TN, 2004, pg. 104

23. *The End of Reason,* by Ravi Zacharias. Zondervan Publishing, Grand Rapids, MI 2008. Pg. 93

24. *The Religions Next Door*, by Marvin Olasky, Broadman and Holman Publishers, Nashville, TN, 2004, pg. 100

25. *The Religions Next Door*, by Marvin Olasky, Broadman and Holman Publishers, Nashville, TN, 2004, pg. 99

26. *The Religions Next Door*, by Marvin Olasky, Broadman and Holman Publishers, Nashville, TN, 2004, pg. 67

27. *The Religions Next Door*, by Marvin Olasky, Broadman and Holman Publishers, Nashville, TN, 2004, pg. 57

28. *The Religions Next Door*, by Marvin Olasky, Broadman and Holman Publishers, Nashville, TN, 2004, pg. 79

29. *The Religions Next Door*, by Marvin Olasky, Broadman and Holman Publishers, Nashville, TN, 2004, pg. 145

30. *What's Right With Islam*, Imam Feisal Abdul Rauf, pg.22, (HarperCollinsSanFrancisco) HarperCollins, New York, NY., 2004

31. Ergun Caner is the President of Liberty Theological Seminary at Liberty University in Lynchburg, Virginia. The website is *erguncaner.com*. He became the first former Muslim to become the leader of an evangelical seminary. Caner has debated Muslims, Hindus, Buddhists and Bah'ai more than sixty times at universities and colleges. He has written fourteen books, including *When Worldviews Collide* (LifeWay 2005), on the subject of Global Apologetics and defending the Christian faith.

32. *1,001 Things You Always Wanted To Know About the Bible, But Never Thought To Ask*, J. Stephen Lang, 1999, Nelson Books, Nashville, TN pg.225.

33. *What's Right With Islam*, Imam Feisal Abdul Rauf, pg.42, (HarperCollinsSanFrancisco) HarperCollins, New York, NY, 2004

34. *What's Right With Islam,* Imam Feisal Abdul Rauf, pg.42, (HarperCollinsSanFrancisco) HarperCollins, New York, NY. pg. 43.

35. *The End of Reason,* by Ravi Zacharias. Zondervan Publishing, Grand Rapids, MI 2008. Pg. 63

36. *The Religions Next Door*, by Marvin Olasky, Broadman and Holman Publishers, Nashville, TN, 2004, pg. 7

37. *Paul, the Spirit and the People of God*, by Gordon D. Fee. Hendrickson Publishers, Inc., Peabody, MA., 1996, reprinted 2007. Pg. 85-86.

38. *Paul, the Spirit and the People of God*, by Gordon D. Fee. Hendrickson Publishers, Inc., Peabody, MA., 1996, reprinted 2007. Pg.161

39. *Paul, the Spirit and the People of God*, by Gordon D. Fee. Hendrickson Publishers, Inc. 1996, Peabody, MA., reprinted 2007. Pg.10.

40. *New Testament Commentary: Romans 1-8*, by John MacArthur, Moody Publishers/Chicago, ILL, 1991, pg. 199

41. *New Testament Commentary: Romans 1-8*, by John MacArthur, Moody Publishers/Chicago, ILL, 1991, pg. 199

42. *The End of Reason,* by Ravi Zacharias. Zondervan Publishing, Grand Rapids, MI. 2008. Pg.63

43. *The End of Reason,* by Ravi Zacharias. Zondervan Publishing, Grand Rapids, MI. 2008. Pg.123

44. *The End of Reason,* by Ravi Zacharias. Zondervan Publishing, Grand Rapids, MI. 2008. Pg.99.

45. Matthew 6:9, The Lord's Prayer, *The Holy Bible*, NIV.

46. *Surprised by Hope*, by N. T. Wright. HarperCollins and HarperOne, New York, NY, 2008. Pg. 198.

47. *New Testament Commentary: Romans 1-8*, by John MacArthur, Moody Publishers/Chicago, ILL. 1991, pg. 198

48. Genesis 1:28 *The Holy Bible* , NIV.

49. *There is A God – How the World's Most Notorious Atheist Changed His Mind*, by Antony Flew with Roy Abraham Varghese, 2007, published by HarperOne, New York, NY. Pg. 138

50. *There is A God – How the World's Most Notorious Atheist Changed His Mind*, by Antony Flew with Roy Abraham Varghese, 2007, published by HarperOne, New York, NY. Pg. 128

51. *There is A God – How the World's Most Notorious Atheist Changed His Mind*, by Antony Flew with Roy Abraham Varghese, 2007, published by HarperOne, New York, NY. Pg. 86

52. Genesis 2:15, The Holy Bible , NIV.

53. Genesis 2:16-17, The Holy Bible , NIV.

54. Genesis 2:20, Holy Bible , NIV

55. Genesis 3:2-3, The Holy Bible , NIV

56. Genesis 3:4-5, The Holy Bible , NIV

57. *New Testament Commentary: Romans 1-8*, by John MacArthur, Moody Publishers/Chicago, ILL. 1991, pg. 184

58. *Surprised by Hope*, by N. T. Wright. HarperCollins and HarperOne, New York, NY. 2008. Pg.280.

59. Quotes from statements made by Prof. Peter Kreeft, professor of Philosophy, Boston College, Boston, MA

60. Quotes from statements made by Prof. Peter Kreeft, professor of Philosophy, Boston College, Boston, MA

61. *New Testament Commentary: Romans 1-8*, by John MacArthur, Moody Publishers/Chicago, ILL. 1991, pg. 189

62. N. T. Wright. Quote taken from *There is A God– How the World's Most Notorious Atheist Changed His Mind*, by Antony Flew with Roy Abraham Varghese, 2007, published by HarperOne, New York, NY Page 207

63. Ezekiel 37:12 (The Holy Bible, NIV) says, *"This is what the Sovereign Lord says; O my people, I am going to open your graves and bring you up from them. I will bring you back to the land of Israel ."*

64. The Vulgate Bible, or that used by Catholics, has books not in the Protestant Bible, Old Testament books such as Baruch, additions to Esther and Daniel, Sirach, Tobit, Judith, Wisdom, 1 Maccabees, 2 Maccabees, and Song of Songs. These are called the Apocrypha. In 2 Maccabees 12:38-46, reference is made to "Expiation for the Dead," which is, as I understand, a foundation for Purgatory. The Jews did not consider these books sacred; thus, they are not included in the Protestant Bible.

65. Hebrews 1:3

66. *The Resurrection of the Son of God* by N. T. Wright, Fortress Press, Minneapolis, MN. 2003.

67. *There is A God – How the World's Most Notorious Atheist Changed His Mind*, by Antony Flew with Roy Abraham Varghese, 2007, published by HarperOne, New York, NY. Pg. 200 (Appendix B)

68. *There is A God – How the World's Most Notorious Atheist Changed His Mind*, by Antony Flew with Roy Abraham Varghese, 2007, published by HarperOne, New York, NY. Pg. 202 (Appendix B)

69. *There is A God – How the World's Most Notorious Atheist Changed His Mind*, by Antony Flew with Roy Abraham Varghese, 2007, published by HarperOne, New York, NY. Pg. 209 (Appendix B)

70. *Rabbi Paul* . Bruce Chilton. Random House, Inc., div. of Doubleday, New York, NY 2004. Pg. 43.

71. *Rabbi Paul* . Bruce Chilton. Random House, Inc., div. of Doubleday, New York, 2004 Pg. 43.

72. *Rabbi Paul* . Bruce Chilton. Random House, Inc., div. of Doubleday, New York, 2004 Pg. 46.

73. Acts 9:2, NIV Bible.

74. Acts 9:5, NIV Bible

75. Acts 9:15. NIV Bible

76. Acts 9:18. NIV Bible

77. *Rabbi Paul* , Bruce Chilton. Random House, Inc., div. of Doubleday, New York, NY. 2004. Page 65

78. Galatians 1:11-20. NIV Bible.

79. *The Faith, What Christians Believe, Why They Believe it, and Why it Matters.* Charles Colson and Harry Fickett. Pg. 92, Zondervan, Grand Rapids, MI 2008.

80. *Surprised by Hope*, by N. T. Wright. HarperCollins and HarperOne, New York, NY 2008. Pg. 157.

81. *Surprised by Hope*, by N. T. Wright. HarperCollins and HarperOne, New York, NY. 2008. Pg.161.

82. Quote of Jesus speaking to his disciples. *The Holy Bible* , NIV. Luke 9:23.

83. *The Imitation of Christ* , author Thomas a'Klempis, rewritten and updated by Harold J. Chadwick, publisher Bridge-Logos, Orlando, FL. Copyright 1999. Orig. written 1427. Page 28

84. *Vatican updates its list of 'thou shalt not' sins*, The Palm Beach Post, Tuesday March 11, 2008, page 2A, from *The Associated Press.*

85. *Humility*, a book by Andrew Murray (1828-1917), a preacher and evangelist in the Dutch Reform Church of South Africa. Copyright 2000 by Bridge-Logos publisher, Orlando, FL.

86. *The Heart of Christianity*, Marcus J. Borg, pg 138, HarperCollins, New York, NY 2003

87. Mosaic Laws; included are the Ten Commandments. See the biblical books Deuteronomy and Leviticus.

88. *The Heart of Christianity*, Marcus J. Borg, HarperCollinsSanFrancisco, Harper Collins, New York, NY 1989, page 112

89. *Major Bible Prophecies*, John F. Walvoord, pg. 188. Zondervan Publishing, Grand Rapids, MI 1991

90. The Last Supper

91. *The Truth of the Cross*, R. C. Sproul, 2007, Reformation Trust Publishing, Lake Mary, Florida. Pg. 39

92. *The Truth of the Cross*, R. C. Sproul. 2007,

Reformation Trust Publishing, Lake Mary, Florida Pg. 47

93. *The Truth of the Cross*, R. C. Sproul. 2007, Reformation Trust Publishing, Lake Mary, Florida Pg. 77

94. *The Truth of the Cross*, R. C. Sproul. 2007, Reformation Trust Publishing, Lake Mary, Florida Pg. 97

95. Zondervan daily words of inspiration – from the internet.

96. The Bible, NIV. Joshua 1:9.

97. *Believing God* , 5 Statement Pledge of Faith, Beth Moore. 2204. Broadmon & Holman publishers, Nashville, TN. Page 30.

98. Online at *Merriam-Webster.com/dictionary/sacrament*

99. The Holy Bible, NIV, 2 Timothy 3:16. *"All Scripture is God breathed and it is useful for teaching, rebuking, correcting and training in righteousness, so that the man of God may be equipped for every good work."*

100. *The Problem of Pain*, C. S. Lewis. 1940, restored 1996. pub. HarperSanFrancisco. Harper Collins, New York, NY. Page 120

101. *New Testament Commentary: Romans 1-8*, by John MacArthur, Moody Publishers/Chicago, ILL. 1991, pg.482

102. Quote from a Sunday Sermon by Steven Woodrow, Crossroads Church , Aspen Colorado, December 30, 2007.

103. *Can Man Live Without God* , Ravi Zacharias, W. Publishing, Nashville, TN. 1994, Word Publishing. Page 150.

104. *Can Man Live Without God* , Ravi Zacharias, W. Publishing, Nashville, TN. 1994, Word Publishing. Page 151

105. Archbishop William Temple , quoted by David Watson in *I Believe in Evangelism* (Grand Rapids, MI, Eerdmans, 1976), pg. 157

106. *Can Man Live Without God* , Ravi Zacharias, W. Publishing, Nashville, TN. 1994, Word Publishing. Page 151

107. *Surprised by Hope*, by N. T. Wright. HarperCollins and HarperOne., New York, NY. 2008. Pg.207

108. *Surprised by Hope*, by N. T. Wright. HarperCollins and HarperOne, New York, NY. 2008. Pg. 193

109. *The Wonder of the World, A Journey from Modern Science to the Mind of God* , Roy Abraham Varghese 2003. Tyr Publishing, Fountain Hills, AZ Page 62

110. "I Can Only Imagine," sung by many music groups, including Mercy Me, and Amy Grant, Counting Crowns.

111. *www .cptryon.org* – Internet site for *Bread on The Waters*.

112. Excerpted from *The Gift of Prayer*, by Victor Hoagland, C.P. based on the New Catholic Catechism 2558-2567, taken from the Internet,

www.cptryon.org. The reference is to Psalm 63:1, which in the NIV Bible reads, "O God, you are my God, earnestly I seek you: my soul thirsts for you, my body longs for you, in a dry and weary land where there is no water."

113. *Dorcas - Acts 9:40:* Tabitha, also known as Dorcas, was a godly woman known for her good works and acts of charity. She is named as a disciple of Jesus, a follower who believed in him. In time, she became sick and died. The widows in the church, as part of their ministry to the body of Christ, prepared her body for burial, washed it, and laid her in an upstairs room. These widows heard that Peter was in the region and so they sent for him. He came right away and when ushered into the room where her body was, and having been shown many of the cloths that she had made for other believers as a testimony to her love for the saints, Peter cleared the room. He then knelt down to pray and then said to the body, "Tabitha, arise." She opened her eyes, saw it was Peter, sat up, and was then presented alive to the saints. News spread and many believed in Jesus because of this miracle. (from the Internet, slightly modified/edited, Web site: *www/pastorway.blogspot.com/2006/04/others-who-were-raised-part-4.html*)

114. *Eutychus - Acts 20:7-12:* In another report of a resurrection, Paul was in Troas and on Sunday he was preaching as the disciples came together to break bread. He was leaving the next day,

and as any preacher, he had lots still to say. As he preached through the night the hour passed midnight. A young man named Eutychus was sitting in the window of this upper room, and as Paul went on, Eutychus fell asleep. (It is nice to see that even the Apostle Paul had people fall asleep while he preached!) However, when he fell asleep, he fell out of the window! He was three stories up, and when they ran to his body he was dead from the fall. Paul went down and fell on him, embracing him. He said that he was alive and as surely as he said it Eutychus was resurrected—he was alive, and so Paul went back up into the room, ate, broke bread, preached some more, and in the morning, left on his journey. This resurrection gave great comfort to the disciples. (from the Internet, slightly modified/edited, Web site: *www/pastorway.blogspot.com/2006/04/others-who-were-raised-part-4.html*)

115. "Worthy is the Lamb," sung by Hillsong United, Album: You Are My World.

116. A quote from Robert Louis Stevenson, 1850-1894

e|LIVE

---

listen|imagine|view|experience

AUDIO BOOK DOWNLOAD INCLUDED WITH THIS BOOK!

In your hands you hold a complete digital entertainment package. Besides purchasing the paper version of this book, this book includes a free download of the audio version of this book. Simply use the code listed below when visiting our website. Once downloaded to your computer, you can listen to the book through your computer's speakers, burn it to an audio CD or save the file to your portable music device (such as Apple's popular iPod) and listen on the go!

How to get your free audio book digital download:

1. Visit www.tatepublishing.com and click on the e|LIVE logo on the home page.
2. Enter the following coupon code: a1c1-db90-5b60-dfa2-40d9-f6cd-f6a8-dc88
3. Download the audio book from your e|LIVE digital locker and begin enjoying your new digital entertainment package today!